Aviation Elite Units

57th Fighter Gro
'First in the Blue'

Aviation Elite Units • 39

57th Fighter Group

'First in the Blue'

Carl Molesworth

Series editor Tony Holmes

Front Cover
The 57th Fighter Group (FG) gained fame for its many notable 'firsts', but its most successful combat mission was the 'Palm Sunday Massacre' of 18 April 1943. As the Luftwaffe was hurrying to evacuate as many troops as possible from Tunisia in the waning days of the North Africa campaign, 48 P-40s of the 57th FG caught a large formation of Ju 52/3m tri-motor transports just off the coast of Cape Bon and swiftly attacked. Capt James G Curl of the 66th FS/57th FG was leading the mission, and he described his part in the action, which resulted in credits for no fewer than 76 enemy aircraft confirmed destroyed;

'I was leading the leader section, lowest cover, flying southwest at 4000 ft. I saw a formation of 75 Ju 52s, escorted by several Me 109s, flying northeast about six miles off the coast. I called a diving turnabout to attack, and as we went down two Me 109s flying tight formation left the rear of the group and started to climb to the southwest. I got in several bursts at both these aircraft from 200-300 yards. I broke off in order to pursue the transports. Lt Cleaveland saw one of the Me 109s nose down and hit the water, thus confirming a destroyed.

'Following the transport formation, I got in several close-range bursts at a Ju 52, and his starboard engine began streaming black smoke and showing signs of being damaged. A second Ju 52 into which I got a close deflection shot twisted violently and pieces of wing flew off.

'The formation headed toward land. I followed a straggler from dead astern and fired several rounds at very close range – he burst into flames and crashed into the water at the beach. Over land I hit one at point-blank range. As he bounced off the ground, one engine burst into flames and he nosed up where he hit, the entire aircraft catching on fire.'

'Big Jim' Curl was credited with one Bf 109 and two Ju 52/3ms destroyed, plus two Junkers tri-motors damaged. Shortly thereafter he was promoted to the rank of major, and on 15 May 1943 was appointed commander of the 66th FS. Curl completed his tour in the summer of 1943, but returned to Italy for a second combat tour in late 1944 as commander of the 2nd FS/52nd FG, flying P-51Ds. Unfortunately, Curl was killed in action on 19 March 1945 (*Cover artwork by Mark Postlethwaite*)

First published in Great Britain in 2011 by Osprey Publishing, Midland House, West Way, Botley, Oxford OX2 0PH, UK
44-20 23rd St, Suite 219, Long Island City, NY 11101, USA

E-mail: info@ospreypublishing.com

© 2011 Osprey Publishing Limited.

A CIP catalogue record for this book is available from the British Library

ISBN: 978 1 84908 337 9
E-book ISBN: 978 1 84908 338 6

Edited by Tony Holmes
Page design by Mark Holt
Cover Artwork by Mark Postlethwaite
Aircraft Profiles by Jim Laurier
Index by Alan Thatcher
Originated by PDQ Digital Media Solutions Ltd
Printed and bound in China through Bookbuilders

11 12 13 14 15   10 9 8 7 6 5 4 3 2 1

Osprey Publishing is supporting the Woodland Trust, the UK's leading woodland conservation charity by funding the dedication of trees.

www.ospreypublishing.com

CONTENTS

INTRODUCTION

This book springs from the research that I did for one of my previous Osprey books, *P-40 Warhawk Aces of the MTO*. The more I learned about the exploits of the 57th FG, the more interested I became in writing the full history of this extraordinary unit.

As a writer, I was intrigued immediately by the slogan of the 57th, 'First in the Blue'. I soon came to realise that the phrase was not only catchy but also full of meaning. The group's list of 'firsts' is lengthy and includes the following – first USAAF unit to deploy to a combat area in group strength from the deck of an aircraft carrier; first USAAF fighter group to go into action in North Africa; first USAAF fighter group to engage the *Regia Aeronautica*; first USAAF fighter group to fight on Sicily; first group to carry two 1000-lb bombs on a P-47; and first USAAF fighter group to complete 4000 missions against the enemy.

Then there is the matter of 'The Blue'. It is logical to assume the term refers to the colour of the sky in which the 57th made its mark in history, and that is certainly true. However, 'The Blue' also was RAF Desert Air Force slang referring to the vast areas of North African desert stretching west from Cairo, where British forces had been slugging it out with the Italians and Germans for two years by the time the 57th arrived in July 1942 to add the firepower of its 72 P-40s to the Allied cause.

In nearly three years of constant combat in the Mediterranean Theatre of Operations (MTO), the 57th FG built an operational record notable not just for its longevity but also for the staggering amount of damage the group inflicted on the Axis forces. Yet the 57th has been overlooked in most recent accounts of US fighter operations during World War 2, which tend to focus primarily on air-to-air combat. The 57th fought numerous air battles over North Africa – with six pilots becoming aces in the process – but the Allies established air superiority over Italy by late 1943 and opportunities for air combat dwindled. The group instead concentrated on fighter-bomber operations, which it pioneered during the desert campaign and developed into one of the Allies' most devastating weapons of the war.

The 57th FG also stands out for the loyalty and *esprit de corps* of its personnel. Most of the ground troops who arrived in North Africa during the summer of 1942 were still with their squadrons to celebrate VE Day nearly three years later. And a surprising number of pilots flew nearly as long, with just a month's leave in mid-war to rest and recuperate before rejoining the fight. In fact, the group commander and all three of the squadron commanders at the end of the war had combat records in the 57th dating back to 1942.

The 57th FG was an outstanding combat unit, a giant among giants in the MTO. I am proud to be able to tell its story.

Carl Molesworth,
Mount Vernon, Washington, USA
October 2010

GROWING PAINS

On the morning of 19 July 1942, Capt C T Durgin, commanding officer of USS *Ranger* (CV 4), watched from the bridge as the big aircraft carrier turned into the wind and prepared to launch aeroplanes from its deck. Launching aircraft was a routine task for *Ranger's* crew, who were then cruising off the Gold Coast of Africa about 150 miles from the airport at Accra in what is now Ghana. Capt Durgin knew this launch, however, had the potential to be anything but routine.

Durgin watched as the pilots of 36 fighters arrived on deck and manned their aeroplanes, while an equal number of aircraft and pilots waited below. But these were not US Navy fighters. They belonged to the US Army Air Force (USAAF), and thus were not designed for carrier operations. Nor were these US Navy pilots. As Durgin knew, nearly all of the USAAF pilots who were to fly the Curtiss P-40F Warhawks that day had never taken off from a carrier deck before, and none had ever made a carrier landing.

Following the plan worked out by Cdr W D Anderson, air officer of the ship, the pilots of the forward 18 fighters started their engines while *Ranger* picked up speed to about 20 knots. Strapped into the cockpit of the first P-40, '01' *Regina IV*, was Maj Frank H Mears, commanding officer of the USAAF pilots. Because of the nose-high stance of the parked P-40, Mears could not see the outstretched deck of *Ranger* in front of him. However, he knew that he had little more than half of the carrier's 700 ft-long flightdeck to get his aeroplane airborne. If he failed, he was going to get wet, or worse.

Mears checked his aeroplane one more time – flaps and trim tabs set, brakes full on. At the signal of the landing signal officer, Mears pushed the throttle full forward, released the brakes and felt his lightly loaded P-40 (110 gallons of fuel and 300 rounds of ammunition) begin to roll. Its tail rose as the forces of aerodynamics kicked in, and almost before he knew it Mears was off the deck and wobbling into the air. He pushed the P-40's nose down to gain speed and avoid stalling, then began a slow, wide circle that would allow time for the other five P-40s in his flight to join up with him prior to heading to Accra.

Next off was 1Lt Roy E Whittaker, who had a reputation as a hot pilot. He did sort of a 'dipsy-doodle' (zig-zag) as he left the deck, and no one who saw it was ever sure whether Whittaker had done the manoeuvre on purpose or not. One by one the rest of the P-40s took off and joined on Mears. When all six aeroplanes were together, Mears led the formation eastward toward land. In less than half-an-hour, all 18 P-40s in the first batch were safely away from *Ranger* and on their way to Africa. Then the second batch of P-40s fired up and took off, again with no problems. So far, so good.

With the deck now clear of aircraft, *Ranger's* crew spent the next hour spotting the third flight of 18 P-40s in preparation for launch. The flight began its take-offs two hours after Mears had departed, and again the USAAF pilots all got away cleanly. The spotting process was repeated one more time for the fourth flight. Finally, some four hours after the first take-off, Capt Archie J Knight's P-40 was the last one left on the carrier. As Knight gunned his aeroplane off the deck safely and headed off toward Africa, Capt Durgin and the crew of *Ranger* gave a collective sigh of relief. All 72 P-40s of the 57th FG were now on their way to war. The 19 July 1942 carrier take-off in group strength was the first of many 'firsts' that the 57th would tally during the coming three years of combat operations.

ACTIVATION

The 57th Pursuit Group (PG) was activated on 15 January 1941 at Mitchell Field, New York. The war in Europe was already in its 17th month by then, and American leaders could see the likelihood of their own nation being drawn into the conflict. US military forces had been badly neglected during the Great Depression of the 1930s, and now a mad dash was beginning to bring them up to strength.

The new group consisted of a headquarters unit and three squadrons, the 64th, 65th and 66th Pursuit Squadrons, each with an authorised strength of 24 aircraft and around 360 personnel. Growth came in fits and starts for the 57th PG during 1941, as men were assigned to the unit directly from training schools and just as rapidly transferred back out, having gained a little experience, to form the nuclei of other new combat units being formed. The first group commander, Capt John E Barr, transferred to the 51st PG on the West Coast in the spring of 1941 and was replaced by Major Reuben Moffat, who previously commanded the 33rd PG. A highly accomplished pilot, Moffat, on 14 October 1940, became the first USAAC pilot to take off from an

The aircraft strength of the 57th PG built up slowly following its activation in January 1941. Here, a pilot and crew chief discuss the condition of a fresh P-40C. Note the unpainted propeller and the plumbing for a drop tank under the belly (*Donald E Williams via Mike Williams*)

aircraft carrier when he flew his P-40 off USS *Wasp* (CV 7) during a test of deployment procedures off the Virginia coast. Moffat moved on in August 1941, replaced by Maj Clayton Hughes, a West Pointer and former cavalry officer who had taken flight training in 1934.

Likewise, the number of P-40s assigned to the group grew slowly over the course of the year. With its sleek lines, 1100-hp Allison V12 engine and machine gun barrels protruding from its nose and wings, the P-40 was the Army's standard frontline fighter of the day. Its speed (nearly 350 mph at 15,000 ft) and somewhat tricky handling characteristics inspired a mixture of pride and respect in the young pilots of the 57th who flew it (see Osprey Duel 8 – *P-40 Warhawk vs. Ki-43 'Oscar'*, for more information about the development of the aircraft).

Although the 57th PG's mission was to provide air defence for the New England area of the United States, in reality it was a training unit during its formative months. The responsibility for getting the 57th's fledgling fighter pilots up to speed fell to a cadre of experienced aviators. Chief among them were Lt Romulus W Puryear, commander of the 64th PS, and Lt Philip G Cochran, his counterpart in the 65th. Other notables were Lts John Alison (a future ace), Harry Pike and Robert Brouk, who would later make their marks while flying in China, plus Capt Peter McGoldrick and Lts Leonard Lydon and Edward Carey, all future fighter group commanders. When Lt Puryear transferred in July 1941 to lead the deployment of the 33rd PS to Iceland, Lt Frank H Mears took command of the 64th PS.

Inevitably, flying accidents occurred during training. On 21 August 1941, two days after the 57th moved to Day Field in Windsor Locks, Connecticut, Lt Eugene M Bradley and Lt Mears were practising combat manoeuvres when Bradley apparently blacked out and spun his P-40C (41-13348) into a stand of dense woods next to the airfield.

A P-40C of the 66th PS makes a stop at Maxwell Field, Alabama, during 1941. In the background is a Douglas OA-3 amphibious transport (*Dan and Melinda Shobe*)

Armourers align the wing guns of 65th PS P-40E 'No 51' (40-383) while the squadron mascot, 'Brownie' the dog, supervises in the foreground. The aeroplane, assigned to Lt Art Salisbury, bears the single fuselage band denoting a flight leader (*Bob Hanning via www.57thfightergroup.org*)

Following his funeral in Hartford, Lt Bradley's remains were interred in the national cemetery in San Antonio, Texas. On 20 January 1942, Day Field was renamed Army Air Base Bradley Field, Connecticut, in his honour. Today, Bradley International Airport is the site of the 57th FG's World War 2 memorial at the New England Air Museum.

By October 1941 the group was considered of sufficient strength and experience to conduct a cross-country exercise. Led by their group commander, Maj Hughes, the 57th PG pilots flew all the way across the nation to McChord Field, Washington, via the southern route. Bad weather and other problems plagued the flight, and the group lost nearly half of its 25 aeroplanes, with four pilots killed in crashes. Thirteen pilots completed the flight and reported to Second Interceptor Command at McChord on 28 October. They flew just one mission from McChord before being ordered to California, where an inquiry into the disastrous flight was to be convened. Further problems ensued, and only ten P-40s had reached March Field by 4 November.

An Aircraft Accident Classification Committee sought not only to determine responsibility for the losses but also to determine means of preventing future problems of this sort. Maj Hughes was not disciplined, although many of the pilots on the flight felt he had made a series of bad decisions as leader, but it is perhaps significant that Hughes was replaced as 57th PG commanding officer a month later,

Pilots and groundcrew of the 65th PS relax on sandbags outside the operations office at Groton, Connecticut. Art Salisbury, deputy squadron commander, is at far left. Ed Silks, intelligence officer, is holding 'Brownie' (*Bob Hanning via www.57thfightergroup.org*)

P-40Es of the 57th PG are parked on the grass beyond a fuel truck and trailer at Groton. Note the protective blast pens in the distance (*Donald E Williams via Mike Williams*)

just days after the Japanese surprise attack on the Pacific Fleet in Pearl Harbor, Hawaii.

With the US now at war, the 57th settled into a steady schedule of air defence patrols and practice missions as its pilots and technicians honed their skills in preparation for deployment to a combat zone. The squadrons were dispersed at various times to airfields at Groton, Connecticut, Quonset Point, Rhode Island, Long Island, New York, and East Boston, Massachusetts. At Groton, the colourful CO of the 65th FS, Capt Phil Cochran, called on his college roommate, cartoonist Milton Caniff, to design a badge for the squadron. They chose a particularly feisty looking rooster wearing a pilot's helmet with a chip on his shoulder and christened the 65th the 'Fighting Cocks'.

The officers of the 65th FS acquired this handsome rooster to serve as the squadron mascot just prior to departing from the US. They assigned two enlisted men to escort the rooster, named 'Uncle Bud', on his deployment by air to the Middle East. He arrived safely and served with the squadron for more than two years before his death (*Donald E Williams via Mike Williams*)

Capt Phil Cochran flew P-40E 'No 50' (41-5726), which he nicknamed *Shillelagh*, in the spring of 1942. The yellow trim on the nose and the 'Fighting Cocks' badge identify it as a 65th PS aircraft, and the twin yellow fuselage bands denote the squadron commander's aircraft (*Bob Hanning via www.57thfightergroup.org*)

Capt Phil Cochran led the 65th PS throughout its formative period but was fated not to make the trip to Egypt. He was hospitalised when the 57th shipped out in July 1942 and subsequently served in the 33rd FG in North Africa and the 1st Air Commando Group in Burma. Cartoonist Milton Caniff, who drew the popular *Terry and the Pirates* comic strip, modelled character 'Flip Corkin' after Cochran (*Francis Hudlow via www.57thfightergroup.org*)

In May 1942, the units' designation officially changed from 'Pursuit' to 'Fighter'.

Finally, on the morning of 24 June 1942 a message arrived at 57th FG headquarters at Quonset Point from the Eastern Defense Command Headquarters, USAAF. The Teletype spat out news that everyone in the unit had been anticipating for months. In the terse language of the military, Special Order No 168 announced that the 57th was going into combat;

'The officers on the attached roster will proceed without delay to Mitchell Field, New York, reporting to the commanding general, I Fighter Command. Upon completion of this temporary duty they will proceed to station outside limits of Continental United States. This is a permanent change of station. Dependents will not accompany any of these officers.'

With the arrival of Special Order No 168, the men of the 57th knew they were on their way overseas. Topping the list of pilots was Maj Frank H Mears, former 64th FS CO, who would serve as group commander. He and 27 other pilots were already members of the 57th FG. The rest were drawn from two other fighter groups, the 33rd and 56th, still in training. Now the big question before the pilots was where they were going.

The answer, or at least a pretty strong hint, awaited them at Mitchell Field. There, the USAAF had assembled 72 brand-new P-40F Warhawks for the 57th FG to take overseas. These aeroplanes differed from the P-40s that the pilots had been flying up to then in two key

ways. Most importantly, P-40Fs were powered by the Packard V-1650-1 Merlin engine, a licence-built version of the now-legendary Rolls-Royce powerplant installed in British Spitfires, Hurricanes and other aircraft. This engine was similar in horsepower and output to the Allison V-1710 installed in earlier (and later) versions of the P-40, but its superior supercharging system allowed it to produce full power at higher altitudes than the American engine could reach.

For another thing, the uppersurface camouflage colour on the P-40Fs was not the ubiquitous Olive Drab that the pilots were accustomed to seeing. These Warhawks were repainted in a colour the USAAF called Desert Tan, but in fact the paint was of a distinctly pinkish hue. Where else could the 57th be going with aircraft painted this way but the desert of North Africa?

June 1942 was a critical month for the British Commonwealth forces fighting in North Africa. Their see-saw war started two years earlier, when Italy declared war on Great Britain in June 1940. The RAF in Egypt immediately launched attacks against the Italians in neighbouring Libya. Emboldened by their German ally's successes in western Europe, the Italians then advanced eastward into Egypt in September 1940. A British counterattack in December pushed them back. Within two months, British forces advanced some 1000 miles to El Agheila, capturing more than 100,000 Italian troops in the process. To head off further disaster, Germany entered the desert war at this point.

German general Erwin Rommel and his soon-to-be-famous *Afrika Korps* attacked in April 1941, and within two weeks the British had

Accidents were inevitable as the young pilots of the 57th PG gained experience. P-40E-1 41-24782, possibly a 65th PS aircraft, sustained only minor damage when its pilot made a belly landing at Groton (*Donald E. Williams via Mike Williams*)

13

been pushed all the way back into Egypt. There a stalemate developed, as German resources were diverted to the Nazi attack on the Soviet Union. The British mounted a second campaign late in the year, and by mid-January 1942 they again were deep inside Libya. But once more, their success was fleeting. Rommel struck back on 26 May 1942 at Gazala, soon pushing British forces all the way back to El Alamein, in Egypt, less than 100 miles from Alexandria.

Just as Rommel's advance was picking up steam, British Prime Minister Winston Churchill arrived in Washington, DC, to discuss war plans with the US president, Franklin D Roosevelt. Early on, the two leaders had agreed on a 'Europe first' policy for the defeat of the Axis powers. American-made war materials were being shipped across the Atlantic at a ferocious pace, but thus far Roosevelt had been reluctant to commit US combat forces to the European conflict piecemeal. He preferred to build up American forces to sufficient strength to open a second front on the continent with one smashing blow. Now, however, with the British backed up in Egypt again and Soviet leader Josef Stalin demanding relief from the German invasion of his country as well, Roosevelt agreed to commit American combat units to North Africa. Among them would be six fighter groups of the USAAF, the first of which was to be operational in-theatre by 1 September 1942. That group would be the 57th FG.

Pilots began arriving at Mitchell Field within 25 hours of receiving Special Order No 168. There, they were surprised to learn that they would be travelling overseas on a US Navy aircraft carrier, and that they would have to fly their P-40s off the ship when they arrived at their

Officers of the 66th FS and their wives have a farewell dinner at Quonset Point, Rhode Island, just prior to going aboard the *Ranger* on 1 July 1942. They are, from left to right, W J 'Jeeter' Yates, next two unidentified, Mrs Dick Paulsen, Dick Paulsen, Dr Mark Conan (flight surgeon), G W 'Bill' Long, Dorothy Long, Pearl Llewellyn and Ray Llewellyn (KIA) (*Dan and Melinda Shobe*)

destination. One of those pilots was 2Lt Dale Deniston, who transferred in from the 33rd FG. He described his short stay at Mitchell in his privately published book, *Memories of a Fighter Pilot*;

'I went up to Mitchell Field on the early morning train. When we arrived at the base, the airfield contained about 75 brand new P-40Fs painted a pink colour, which we guessed might be desert camouflage. We were processed with shots and given both dental and physical exams. Having drawn sidearms, winter flying gear and all sorts of other stuff, we met our aeroplanes – mine was "No 84". All aircraft were brand new, with only four hours total engine and flight time.

'Prior to flying the aircraft, several US Navy pilots instructed us on how to perform carrier take-offs. They painted lines on the runway to indicate about 1000 ft. We were to set flaps, set trim tabs to compensate for torque, run the engine up to full power, hold the stick back and then release brakes. Into the wind, I think the least distance we were able to get airborne was 1200 ft!

'We flew several squadron flights from Mitchell, and on the final one we didn't come back. Instead, we were directed to Quonset Point Naval Air Station. As I circled for landing at Quonset Point, I spotted an aircraft carrier in port. After landing, sailors along the runway directed me to taxi off down a road right to the dock. I taxied up to the dock next to the carrier and was given the sign to cut the engine. As I sat in the cockpit filling out my Form I report, sailors were climbing all over my aircraft and removing my engine cowling.

'A sailor said, "Lieutenant, you will have to get out now as we are taking it aboard". The hoist came down, was attached to the engine mount and my bird was taken up to the flightdeck of USS *Ranger*. Soon all the aircraft and pilots (including six alternate pilots in case of illness) were aboard, and we were at sea, destination unknown.'

The 57th's carrier deployment was not unprecedented, as *Ranger* had delivered a shipment of 68 P-40E-1s to Accra, on the Gold Coast of Africa, in late May 1942. These aircraft were then ferried across Africa and the Middle East to India, where they served as replacements in the 51st FG. Some of them even went on to fly combat in China. The 57th FG would not be going quite that far, as the pilots learned shortly after *Ranger* put to sea. But the 57th would be the first USAAF group to deploy via carrier as a unit, and it too would fly off *Ranger* to Accra, but its destination was Egypt. Here, it would operate in the RAF's Desert Air Force (DAF). First, however, was the matter of taking off from a US Navy carrier in a USAAF fighter not known for its climbing

Tan P-40Fs of the 57th FG share deck space with US Navy dive-bombers aboard *Ranger* as the ship prepares to leave Quonset Point for Africa in early July 1942. The forward half of the deck was cleared when the ship arrived off the African coast to allow room for the P-40s to take-off (*New England Air Museum*)

Some pilots chose to decorate their P-40s during the sea voyage aboard the *Ranger*. Here, Lt Richard Kimball paints the name of his girlfriend on the cowling of his 'No 56'. Kimball, flying in the 65th FS, would be shot down on 20 January 1943 by Leutnant Reinert of II/JG 77 (*New England Air Museum*)

performance. 2Lt Bill Mount of the 64th FS recalled his departure from *Ranger*;

'We had tried practice take-offs at Mitchell Field and had gotten off in between 1150 ft and 1300 ft into a 20-knot wind. The US Navy told us the deck was 750 ft long, and heading into the wind made a big difference. It was only after we were aboard and learned that the aft half of the deck was full of P-40s that we were told we would only be allowed to use the front half of the flightdeck – 350 ft. That's when we got a little worried.

'I took off between 30th and 40th. Only Roy Whittaker's ship made a dip off the end of the flightdeck, and since he was a pretty good showman we thought he did it on purpose. We had been required to run all our trim tab controls to both extreme positions every day during

Lt Marshall Sneed and Capt Charles Fairlamb get some exercise by pulling through the propeller of 66th FS P-40F 'No 85' on the flightdeck of the *Ranger*. Note how the sand-coloured paint has failed to cover a strip of Olive Drab on the fighter's lower cowling (*New England Air Museum*)

Maj Frank Mears, 57th FG commanding officer, briefs his pilots on carrier take-off procedures and the flight plan for reaching the African coast from the *Ranger*. Mears, standing at left with his back to the camera, must have given a good briefing because all 72 P-40Fs of the group reached Africa safely (*New England Air Museum*)

the voyage in order to avoid corrosion. As a result, when I went up to take-off, I had forgotten to reset the tabs. The aeroplane was trimmed full tail heavy and full left rudder. I spent the take-off roll trying to adjust tabs and fighting the controls. We had also covered the canopies with some stuff to eliminate sun reflections. In the damp climate off the Nigerian coast, condensation mixed with the goop so it was impossible to see out with the canopy closed, so I left it open. I probably started becoming deaf at that point.

'Landing at Accra was no problem, as the runway was long and wide. We did damage a few with ground loops, however (not me). We had loaded a few rounds of ammunition because some of the territory we were to fly over was Vichy French – not friendly. The rest of the ammunition boxes were filled with cigarettes.'

The P-40s only stayed at Accra long enough to refuel. Then, with RAF bombers leading, they pressed on eastward in smaller flights, reaching Lagos by evening. Over the next week-and-a-half they made their way across the continent in hops of 100 to 300 miles. By 1 August they had reached Muqueibila, in Palestine, where the group spent several weeks learning how to fight in the desert, RAF-style.

Meanwhile, the ground personnel of the 57th FG had been split into two groups. A small advance echelon of 42 technicians was flown

Lt John E Teichrow prepares to take-off from the *Ranger* in his P-40F 'No 77' *LUCY* on 19 July 1942, bound for Accra on the African Gold Coast. Teichrow would go on to fly throughout the North African campaign, claiming a Bf 109 damaged on 13 March 1943 (*New England Air Museum*)

Lts Dick Paulsen and Roy Whittaker collect pineapples during a stop at Lagos, West Africa, in July 1942 while ferrying their P-40Fs across the continent toward Egypt (*Dick Paulsen*)

Sudanese guards pose with Lt Frank Hertzberg's P-40F 'No 55' (41-13969) at Khartoum while the 57th FG's aircraft were en route to Egypt in July 1942. Note the fighter has not yet been decorated with the red propeller spinner that was a standard marking of the RAF's DAF (*Frank Hertzberg*)

directly from the US to Palestine, arriving on 14 July 1942, to prepare for the arrival of the group's aircraft. One such individual was Cpl Bill Hahn, an armourer in the 65th FS, who recalls having an additional duty during his long journey by air from Miami, Florida, to Palestine;

'There were seven C-47 cargo aeroplanes on the ramp. We were assigned 21 men to each aeroplane. My name and a fellow corporal, Herb Jorisch, were instructed to report to Lt Silks (squadron intelligence officer). He handed us a Rhode Island red rooster whom he called "Uncle Bud", stating this was the squadron mascot, and we were to chaperone this bird to Cairo. Herb and I could have wrung "Bud's" neck many times during the flights. He went among the men pecking at their legs, and when airborne he would flap his wings and try to crow, but over 10,000 ft he lost his crow. What a frustrated bird he was. We delivered "Bud" to our final destination in good health and in one piece. He lived a good life among the squadron men, being occasionally allowed an Egyptian hen to play with. "Bud" was finally killed by a Jeep in Grosseto, Italy, on 29 September 1944. He was given a proper burial.'

The remaining groundcrew travelled by ship across the Atlantic, around Africa and up the Red Sea, arriving in Palestine on 19 August. At the same time, the USAAF's fledgling Ninth Air Force, which would command American air power in the desert, was getting organised in Cairo as a subordinate unit of the DAF.

With combat-experienced RAF pilots serving as instructors, the 57th began a series of practice missions. The British pilots were impressed with the flying skills of their new American allies, many of whom had hundreds of hours of P-40 time, and immediately began training them in their new role, that of fighter-bombers. Over the past two years the DAF had developed tactics that expanded the capabilities of its fighter force by employing it primarily against Axis ground targets in the desert. The fighters served as long-range artillery, sweeping behind Axis lines to destroy communication and supply routes or attacking enemy ground forces directly on the battlefield. If enemy aircraft were encountered, the fighters could jettison their bombs and protect

The 66th FS lived in this tent camp at Beit Darrus, in Palestine, during early August 1942 while preparing to go into combat (*Herb Gluckman*)

The men of the 57th FG were able to take time for some sight-seeing when they reached Egypt. Here, Lt Bill Long of the 66th FS poses in front of the Sphinx as a pyramid stands in the background (*Dan and Melinda Shobe*)

A very confident looking Lt Col Frank H Mears strikes a pose in August 1942 after leading his 57th FG from the comforts of stateside service to the sparse landscape of a landing ground in the Egyptian desert west of Cairo. Mears would command the group during the final advance from El Alamein before accepting a transfer to Ninth Air Force headquarters in December 1942 (*New England Air Museum*)

themselves. Typically, the DAF formation performing a fighter-bomber mission would divide itself, using half its strength as an assault flight and the other half as top-cover escort. Of course, the fighters were also used for more traditional tasks, such as fighter sweeps, interceptions and bomber escorts.

The P-40 was particularly well suited for this role. Never the best performing fighter in the sky, it was nevertheless reliable, carried heavy armament and could withstand amazing amounts of battle damage and still bring its pilot home safely. The Merlin-powered P-40Fs of the 57th FG were fitted with six 0.50-cal machine guns, and they also boasted attachment points under the wings and centreline that allowed them to carry an assortment of light and heavy bombs. Although the aeroplane's climb performance was sluggish and its combat effectiveness limited to low and medium altitudes up to about 20,000 ft, it was more manoeuvrable than either the German Bf 109 or Italian C.202 fighters that it would face. The P-40 was also a spectacular diver.

From the RAF, the green pilots of the 57th FG learned that air-to-air combat tactics in the desert were not much removed from those used over the Western Front during World War 1 – keep your head on a swivel and always 'beware of the Hun in the sun'. Attacks were likely to come from above, with Axis pilots converting the superior altitude capabilities of their aircraft into speed in a diving attack. The best defence, RAF Kittyhawk pilots had learned, was to turn into the attack and bring the P-40's heavy firepower to bear in a head-on pass. It was a tactic the pilots of the 57th FG would depend on time and time again in the difficult months to come.

FIRST IN THE BLUE

Small groups of 57th FG pilots began moving up to the front lines in Egypt during August 1942 to gain actual combat experience with the DAF. These pilots, initially unit commanders and flight leaders, were assigned to Kittyhawk and Tomahawk squadrons. They would fly as wingmen to combat veterans during their first fighter-bomber sorties over the Western Desert – or in DAF parlance, 'The Blue'. Here, in the barren lands west of the Nile River, they would fight for the next nine months.

It was on these makeshift landing grounds just east of El Alamein, and about 100 miles west of the Egyptian port city Alexandria, that the pilots and groundcrews got their first taste of desert life. It was not, perhaps, what they expected.

Rather than the flowing sand dunes they had seen in *National Geographic* magazine, the land here on the coastal plain was featureless and hard. A landing ground was merely a flat spot cleared of rocks, with four 55-gallon drums defining the boundaries of the runway, a wind sock in the middle and villages of tents off to the sides where the men lived and worked. There were no permanent buildings and no revetments. The only paved surface was the narrow coastal highway that ran nearby. Water was as scarce as flies were plentiful. In fact, one veteran of this period told the author that the best way to spot someone who had been in the desert for a long time was to watch him eat. If the man could get a piece of food into his mouth without swallowing a fly, he had been in 'The Blue' long enough to develop the skill.

The crude conditions would harden the Americans rapidly. Although perhaps not as unmilitary as the pilots who flew in China in Claire Chennault's American Volunteer Group, 57th FG personnel became similarly irregular in regard to uniforms and military bearing. If anything, they were more unkempt than the AVG pilots because the shortage of water made bathing and washing clothes a luxury. There also was an element of danger just being on a desert landing ground, because there was nowhere to hide during enemy air attacks. Slit trenches hacked out of the rocky soil offered scant protection from flying bullets and bomb fragments.

A formation of P-40Fs from the 66th FS, recently arrived from the US, makes a low pass over a desert landing ground. During the 57th's initial combat missions, pilots flew their aircraft with experienced DAF Kittyhawk squadrons. Indeed, the 'Fluid Six' formation seen here was adopted by the group from the RAF's No 239 Wing (*Wayne Dodds collection*)

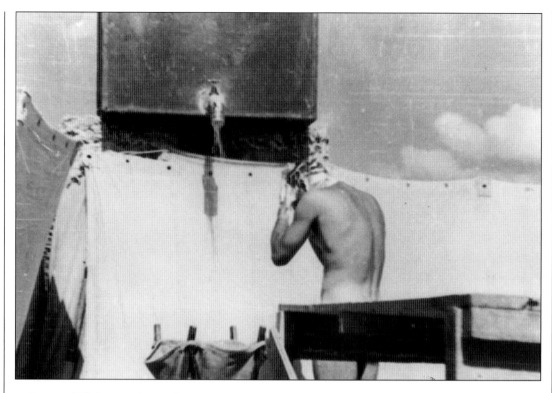

On top of all that was the weather. No one was surprised to find the desert blazing hot and dry, but they soon learned it could also become cold and damp. Adding to that were the frequent dust storms, when huge clouds of sand would blow up from the south and shut down everything for days at a time. With visibility at zero and stinging sand flying everywhere, there was nothing the men could do during these storms but sit in their tents and wait them out.

The 64th FS found inspiration in one of the most persistent pests encountered in 'The Blue'. The men quickly learned to beware of black scorpions – predatory arthropod animals with a nasty stinger on their tail – invading their tents at night. It became common practice for the men to shake out their boots each morning to avoid being stung. Someone decided 'Black Scorpions' would be a good nickname for the squadron, and before long the 64th FS P-40s were sporting representations of the nasty insect on their radiator cowlings.

Gerald Schwartz, a crew chief in the 66th FS, recalled a special visitor of that period who made a poor impression on the American servicemen;

'The rest of the squadron had joined the advanced cadre at Mariut, a suburb of Alexandria. With the RAF supplying guidance, our pilots learned formation and combat tactics and were deemed ready to take on the Luftwaffe.

'One day a strange, small aircraft landed, and it piqued our curiosity because we had never seen anything like it. It was a Fieseler Storch, a captured Luftwaffe single-engined light aeroplane that could land and take off utilising a small runway. Two men exited it and walked towards our operations tent and that of the RAF. When they approached, we all recognised one of them. It was Wendell Willkie, who in 1940 had lost

Water was a scarce and prized commodity in 'The Blue'. Here, one of the men takes advantage of a rare opportunity to take a shower and wash his hair. Note the fabric basin for catching runoff so that the dirty water could be used for another purpose (*Dan and Melinda Shobe*)

Dust storms were a recurring hazard of desert life for machines as well as men. After the first bad storm experienced by the 57th FG on 4 September 1942, 66th FS crew chief Herb Gluckman reported in his diary, 'We have to take all precautions to keep the dust from getting in the engines. It gets all over' (*Lou Lederman*)

the election for president of the United States. President Roosevelt had loaned him a B-24 Liberator bomber so he could travel around the world as the President's emissary. Willkie had referred to the trip as part of his 'One World' philosophy.

'Our armament officer, a young lieutenant, ran forward with his arm outstretched to shake Mr Willkie's hand, but the latter merely ignored him, turned away, and entered the RAF's operations building. The lieutenant was dumbstruck and just stood there not believing what had just happened. Here we are, the only Americans in-theatre, with the "stars and stripes" flying from the mast on our tent, and Mr Willkie snubbed us, and walked toward the one with the Union Jack instead.'

The 57th FG's first orientation missions took place on 9 August 1942. The American pilots' first encounter with enemy aircraft came five days later. On the morning of 14 August 1942, six pilots of the 57th FG were assigned to fly with No 260 Sqn of the RAF while providing top cover for 12 South African Air Force (SAAF) Boston bombers attacking Fuka Station.

As the formation crossed the front lines near El Alamein, 14 Bf 109s attacked from out of the sun and a whirling dogfight ensued. 1Lt William W O'Neill Jr of the 65th FS, flying on the wing of ace Sgt Ron Cundy, spotted a Bf 109 below him to the right and broke off to attack it. He soon found himself overwhelmed by five more Bf 109s, and after a brief but fierce fight was shot down and bailed out over the Mediterranean Sea. O'Neill landed close to shore and was able to inflate his dinghy and paddle to the beach in Allied-held territory. Upon returning to his unit O'Neill reported that he had destroyed two Bf 109s, but his claims were never recognised.

The first accepted USAAF claim in the MTO came on 4 September 1942, when 2Lt Thomas T Williams of the 66th FS was credited with one Bf 109 probably destroyed. Williams was flying top cover with No 260 Sqn on a morning escort mission near El Alamein when the formation was attacked by several Bf 109s and C.202s. The enemy fighters came in from the north and made a run at the middle cover flight, leaving themselves vulnerable to the top cover P-40s. Lt Williams, in P-40F 'No 77', got a shot at one of the Bf 109s and saw his fire hitting home before he was forced to break off the engagement. A C.202 was destroyed by an RAF pilot before the enemy fighters fled the area.

According to Maj Porter R Chandler, 66th FS intelligence officer, 'Lt Williams at the time reported his attack but was unable to state the results. Some days later word was received that a tail gunner of one of the escorted bombers had seen the encounter and had seen the enemy aeroplane go down. Unfortunately, our field telephone line went dead and stayed dead just as we were attempting to get further confirmation sufficient to turn the "probable" into a "destroyed".'

By 13 September 1942 the pilots of the 57th FG had completed 158 sorties with their host RAF and SAAF squadrons. With training and orientation to the desert now complete, the time had come to reunite the 57th FG so it could begin operating as a unit. On 16 September, personnel from group headquarters and the three squadrons – the 64th, 65th and 66th FSs – began converging on LG 174, their new home.

At first, each of the 72 pilots was assigned to a specific P-40, usually the one he flew off the *Ranger*. Many of these aeroplanes were adorned with personal markings, such as nicknames, pilot/crew names and artwork, which was usually on the rudder. Soon they would be adding

Lt Thomas T Williams of the 66th FS (fourth from left) opened the scoring for the 57th FG on 4 September 1942 when he was credited with a Bf 109 probably destroyed while escorting bombers. His squadronmates are, from left to right, Tom Boulware, Mark Conan (flight surgeon), G W 'Pop' Long, Williams, Albert Zipser, Ralph Baker, Lewis Bowen, Dick Paulsen, John Teichrow, Rob Looney, Jim Curl and Dale Deniston (*Dan and Melinda Shobe*)

victory markings as well. But it was not always possible for a pilot to fly 'his' P-40 on a sortie due to flight schedules, aircraft maintenance and repairs and, of course, the occasional loss of an aircraft in combat. Later, when replacement pilots began to arrive toward the end of 1942, the new men would have to wait until they gained some combat experience before being assigned a personal P-40.

The 57th FG began flying missions as part of the RAF's No 211 Group, gaining full operational status on 7 October 1942. Two days later, the Warhawk pilots recorded their first confirmed aerial victory. Six P-40Fs of the 64th FS, led by the unit's commanding officer, Maj

The P-40 quickly earned a reputation for toughness that was greatly appreciated by 57th FG pilots. On 29 September 1942, Maj Charles Fairlamb of the 66th FS flew Warhawk 'No 91' back to LG 174 with a man-sized hole in the left wing, obtained during a skirmish with Bf 109s. Here, Sgt Bill Tilson pokes his head though the damaged wing tip as Carl Volter and Leslie Moulton look on (*Gerald E Smith*)

The 57th FG quickly adapted to the dusty conditions associated with desert landing grounds. Here, the crew chief rides on the wing of a 64th FS P-40F to direct the pilot around obstacles as he taxis into position to take off. Note the sharksmouth painted onto the P-40's drop tank (*Lyle Custer*)

Lt Bill Mount of the 64th FS (centre, looking over his sunglasses) was credited with the first confirmed victory scored by the 57th FG after he shot down a Bf 109 over LG 104 on 9 October 1942. 64th FS officers posing with him here are (from left to right) Don Volker, R J 'Rocky' Byrne, Bill Ottoway, Pete Mitchell (armaments officer), Carl Nelson (intelligence officer), Mount, Fred Ryan (engineering officer), R J 'Jay' Overcash, Tom Tilley, George Mobbs and Glade 'Buck' Bilby (*Bill Mount*)

Lt Arnold Jaqua was the first 65th FS pilot credited with a claim against an enemy aircraft, downing a Bf 109 and damaging a second fighter on 13 October 1942 in P-40F 'No 47' *Sally*. Jaqua was later shot down and killed, 65th FS personnel finding his grave when the unit reached Gabes in March 1943 (*Bob Hanning via www.57thfightergroup.org*)

Clermont 'Pudge' Wheeler, were escorting 18 Boston bombers attacking the enemy airfield at El Daba when the action occurred. One of the pilots flying with Maj Wheeler was 1Lt William J Mount, who recalled the mission more than 50 years later;

'I was pretty lucky to get the first aerial victory in our unit. I was flying on Bob Barnum's wing, and we were to get the Germans to fly their aeroplanes if we could. This usually resulted in them having lots of maintenance problems. Also, there had been light rain the night before, which left their field muddy. Barnum saw something and did a quick half-roll and split-S that I could not follow. About that time I saw this lone Bf 109 fly across in front of me heading out to sea. I was above him and he was climbing. I tacked onto his tail, diving slightly and caught up with him, gave him a long burst and saw the aeroplane disintegrate, breaking in two behind the cockpit. It fell into the ocean. By then I was on my own and, as I recall, proceeded to return to base.'

Mount would go on to fly 95 missions, claiming one further enemy aircraft damaged, before completing his combat tour and returning to the US in May 1943.

Four days after Mount's success, P-40s of the 57th FG got into a scrap with 20 Bf 109s over El Alamein. In this engagement, Lt Arnold D Jaqua recorded the first claims for the 65th FS – one Bf 109 destroyed and another damaged. Now all three squadrons of the 57th FG 'were on the board'.

BATTLE OF EL ALAMEIN

Late in the evening of 23 October 1942, the heavy artillery of Lt Gen Bernard L Montgomery's British 8th Army opened fire against German positions along the 40-mile front at El Alamein. Troops had been massing on both sides of the front, which stretched southward from the beaches of the Mediterranean Sea to the impassable Qatarra Depression, for seven weeks since the British had halted the most recent thrust by Rommel's *Afrika Korps*. Now the decisive battle of the two-year-old war in the desert was about to begin.

At first light on 24 October, some 230,000 men of the 8th Army began moving forward in three distinct thrusts against the 107,000 Italian and German troops facing them. Above the front, creating an umbrella over the Allied troops and a hailstorm of bombs and bullets for the enemy, were massed formations of DAF bombers and fighters. No 211 Group boasted seven Kittyhawk squadrons and one Tomahawk squadron, plus three squadrons each of Spitfires, Hurricanes and 57th FG Warhawks. A further eight Hurricane squadrons flew in No 212 Group, and nine bomber squadrons were equipped with Bostons, Baltimores and USAAF B-25 Mitchells. The primary Axis fighter forces opposing the Allied pilots were the three *gruppen* of the Luftwaffe's legendary JG 27 and one of JG 53, all flying Bf 109F/Gs, plus seven Italian *gruppi* equipped with C.202s.

The P-40F Warhawks of the 57th FG flew no fewer than three missions on 24 October, each time escorting Boston bombers, but had only one inconsequential encounter with enemy fighters during the day. A midday mission by the 64th FS on 25 October brought the initial victory for the pilot who would become the 57th FG's first ace, 1Lt Lyman Middleditch Jr, a 27-year-old New Yorker who had joined the squadron a few days before the *Ranger* deployment.

Middleditch was flying P-40F 'No 17' in a formation of eight P-40s assigned to attack LG 20, a known Bf 109 base. On arrival over the target, mission leader Capt Glade 'Buck' Bilby noted dust rising from the airstrip but no aircraft parked there. Obviously, enemy fighters had just taken off, so Bilby led his formation in a diving attack on a concentration of motor transports parked at the edge of the field.

The enemy aircraft most often encountered by the 57th FG during the desert campaign was the Bf 109. This one, found in November 1942 abandoned when the group reached LG 106 in western Egypt, is an F-model that appears to have been flown by a *staffelkapitan* from JG 27 (*Herb Gluckman*)

Shortly after the P-40s had released their bombs, five or more Bf 109s attacked them. The 64th FS mission report takes up the story;

'Lt Middleditch saw two Me 109s on Lt (Ernest D) Hartman's tail, made a right turn and gave the enemy aeroplane a good burst. The enemy aeroplane went into the sea.'

Lt Middleditch's victory was confirmed by three pilots who saw the Bf 109 go down.

Two days later, Lt Middleditch achieved one of the most spectacular successes in the early history of the 57th FG when he despatched three Bf 109s in a single mission while flying in an eight-aeroplane 64th FS formation providing top cover for eight 65th FS fighter-bombers. Shortly after the P-40s delivered their bombs on LG 20, a large formation of Stukas was spotted heading in from the west, a flight of four Bf 109s was seen approaching from the opposite direction and a third enemy gaggle was observed heading southward from over the sea. Middleditch's flight attacked one of the Bf 109 formations, and he hit a German fighter on his first pass, causing it to smoke. He then dove behind another Bf 109, but his excessive speed caused his shots to miss the target.

Now at low altitude, and wrestling to regain control of his P-40F ('No 13'), Middleditch got a glimpse of his first victim crashing into the ground before he was attacked by three more Bf 109s as he crossed over the coastline. The future ace began turning into the attacks of the enemy machines as they closed on him one after the other, firing at them when he had a chance. He hit the first Bf 109 with a telling burst, and it splashed into the sea. The other two kept up their attacks, and he was finally able to close in on one of them and hit it solidly in the middle of the fuselage. The fighter half-rolled and then cart-wheeled into the water. Now Middleditch only had two guns firing. He continued to turn with the last Bf 109 until the German pilot lost his nerve and broke off the combat, allowing Middleditch to return safely to LG 174.

A few weeks later, Maj Gen Lewis H Brereton, Ninth Air Force commander, and AVM Arthur Coningham, DAF commander, made a surprise visit to the 57th FG. According to group lore, the unit's personnel were quickly rounded up for a decorations ceremony, in which Lt Middleditch was to be awarded the Distinguished Service Cross (DSC) in recognition of his combat success. The motley group of desert warriors included cooks in aprons, mechanics in grease-stained

AVM Arthur Coningham, DAF commander, awarded the DSC to Lt Lyman Middleditch in a surprise ceremony at Gambut on 11 November 1942, shortly after the 64th FS pilot had shot down three Bf 109s on 27 October. Middleditch went on to become the 57th FG's first ace when he shot down his fifth enemy aircraft on 4 April 1943 (*Wayne Dodds collection*)

coveralls and even some men stripped to the waist. Lt Middleditch, who had been helping some mechanics working on a P-40 at the time, hopped down from astride a partially dismantled Merlin engine and took his place in the front row. When the general approached him, he stepped forward and saluted smartly, only noticing later that a roll of toilet paper was protruding from a pocket in his pants!

In his diary, Gen Brereton indicated that the medal was awarded to Lt Middleditch for becoming the 'first ace' of the Ninth Air Force. An extensive search of 57th FG records has only turned up credits for four enemy aeroplanes destroyed by Lt Middleditch up to this date, but the general turned out to be correct nevertheless. When the young pilot scored again on 2 April 1943, no one else in the Ninth Air Force had yet reached five victories.

The future leading ace of the 57th FG also scored his first confirmed victory over the El Alamein front. 1Lt Roy E 'Deke' Whittaker, a 23-year-old native of Knoxville, Tennessee, had joined the USAAC in the spring of 1941 and earned his pilot's wings just five days after the Pearl Harbor attack. He served as a flight instructor for a short period before joining the 65th FS in New England. Whittaker saw combat for the first time on 13 August 1942, flying in an RAF Kittyhawk formation that bombed and strafed tents and trucks south of El Alamein.

Lt Whittaker completed his 13th combat mission on the morning of 26 October, escorting bombers and encountering no aerial opposition. Then at 1425 hrs that same day he was up again in his P-40F 'No 43' *Miss Fury!* when the 65th FS was scrambled to intercept an incoming air raid. Whittaker's flight, led by Capt Thomas W Clark, attacked Italian C.202s south of El Daba and came away with four victories. Capt Clark was credited with two confirmed destroyed and Lts Whittaker and Robert Metcalf got one apiece. Lt Whittaker scored again near El Daba the following day during an encounter with Italian CR.42 biplane fighters, getting one confirmed, one probable and one damaged.

During this period, the 66th FS was separated from its parent group and assigned to the RAF's No 233 Wing, flying out of LG 91. It was from here that 2Lt R Johnson 'Jay' Overcash took off on the morning of 28 October for an escort mission with his unit and returned after having notched his first victory. The formation was jumped by Bf 109s, and Overcash knocked one down for his squadron's only claim of the mission. Following a transfer to the 64th FS, Overcash claimed four more victories to reach 'acedom'. A late afternoon mission that same day netted one confirmed victory apiece for 66th FS pilots Capt Raymond A Llewellyn, 1Lt Robert M Adams, who became a PoW on 4 November when he was shot down by flak, and 2Lt Thomas M Boulware, who was later killed in action.

The last future ace to claim his first victory during the struggle at the El Alamein front was 2Lt Robert J 'Rocky' Byrne of the 64th FS. Byrne, a former professional baseball player from St Louis, Missouri, had arrived in Egypt in August to join the 64th FS. On 30 October 1942, he was assigned to fly P-40F 'No 13' (the same aeroplane in which Lt Middleditch had scored his three kills on 27 October) on a dive-bombing mission along the coast.

With 12 Warhawks of the 65th as top cover, Maj Clermont Wheeler led the 64th FS ten miles out to sea before turning southeast toward the target at 13,000 ft. Reaching the coast, Wheeler spotted the building he was assigned to attack and peeled off to begin his bomb run, with his seven Warhawks close behind. The bombs were released at 8000 ft, none hitting the target, and then six Bf 109s attacked the 64th FS head-on.

Maj Wheeler and Capt Richard E Ryan snapped off bursts at the leading Bf 109s as they passed, getting credit for one damaged and one probably destroyed, respectively. Lt Byrne also came under attack and fired at a passing Bf 109, but saw no hits. He then spotted three more Messerschmitts below him and dove to attack them. He closed in behind one of the Bf 109s and opened fire, then watched as the stricken aeroplane hit the ground, with one wing tearing off as the rest of the wreckage burst in flames. The other two German fighters fled for safety, and Lt Byrne returned to LG 174.

Not so lucky was 1Lt Gordon Ryerson, who damaged a Bf 109 in the scrap before taking hits in the engine, cockpit and tail section of his P-40F 'No 32'. Wounded in one hand and struggling with damaged controls, Lt Ryerson was only able to make left turns. Somehow, he managed to fly the Warhawk home to LG 174, but the fighter flipped over on landing and had to be written off. Lt Ryerson survived the wreck and returned to combat flying, only to subsequently be killed in action.

By 4 November it had become clear to General Rommel that the *Afrika Korps* faced destruction if it did not disengage from Montgomery's attacking 8th Army at El Alamein. Much to the

On 4 November 1942 the 66th FS suffered its first combat loss after flying 71 missions comprising more than 600 sorties. Lt Robert Adams, flying his P-40F 'No 83' *Swampus Cat*, was shot down by ground fire behind enemy lines while escorting bombers. The group received word in January 1943 that Adams was a prisoner of the Italians (*Norman Brandman*)

displeasure of his superiors in Berlin, Rommel ordered his forces to begin an orderly retreat westward. Thus began the next phase of war in 'The Blue' – a 1400-mile chase across Libya and Tunisia that would continue until the following spring. Rommel, for all his brilliance as a tactician and field commander, had simply not been able to overcome the sheer weight of numbers commanded by Montgomery. Similarly, the vaunted JG 27 collapsed under pressure from Allied aerial attacks. Already depleted in aircraft and experienced pilots at the beginning of the El Alamein campaign after two years of constant combat over the desert, JG 27 was withdrawn from Africa and replaced by JG 77, fresh from the Eastern Front.

During the fighting over El Alamein, pilots of the 57th FG scored a total of 27 confirmed victories, five probables and 12 damaged while losing just a handful of P-40s. More importantly, they had matured as a combat team and mastered the fighter-bomber tactics of the DAF. Before the end of the North African campaign, the 57th FG would move some 34 times to new airfields as the Allied advance pressed farther west, completing the trek at Cape Bon, Tunisia, in June 1943.

With Rommel's *Afrika Korps* now in full retreat in Western Egypt, the DAF threw everything it had at the German and Italian forces during the last two months of 1942. As the front moved steadily westward, the Allied fighter units followed closely behind in order to keep their aircraft within range of their targets. By the second week of November, the 57th FG had already moved twice. Indeed it was now beyond the Egyptian border, operating from landing grounds at Gambut, in Libya.

The 57th FG learned how to move quickly during the rapid advance from El Alamein. Here, the 66th FS convoy has been halted by a mine explosion while travelling along the coastal road through Libya in December 1942. The squadron groundcrews split into A and B groups, which would leap-frog each other as they moved to advanced landing grounds near the frontline (*Norman Brandman*)

The armament section of the 65th FS arrives at a new landing ground in Libya. The armourers built this rolling shop to keep their tools and equipment organised during their frequent moves across 'The Blue' (*Bob Hanning via www.57thfightergroup.org*)

A P-40F of the 66th FS gets an engine change outdoors at a desert landing ground. The P-40Fs' Merlin engines wore out quickly in the desert due to the dusty conditions, despite extreme measures taken by the crew chiefs to keep the powerplants buttoned up when the planes were on the ground (*Gerald E Smith*)

The complex logistics involved in moving the squadrons fell on the shoulders of the hard-working ground personnel. Borrowing again from RAF tactics, each American squadron divided into A and B groups. Both groups consisted of enough mechanics and armourers to keep the squadron operational. While A Group was servicing the P-40s, B Group would move forward to the next base and prepare it for operations. Then when the P-40s moved to B Group's location, A Group would go yet farther forward, and the leap-frog process would begin again.

One of the men who took part in these leap-frog operations was Sgt Lyle Custer, an armourer in the 64th FS. On 9 November 1942 he made this diary entry;

'Today we went on another 100 miles closer to the front. There were a lot of wrecked German tanks and trucks, and a few dead bodies, along the road. Saw a lot of wrecked aeroplanes on aerodromes, most of them German but a few British too. There are a lot of minefields. Some of the towns we went through were Bir-El Arab and Daba. Most of the towns are only piles of stones. We saw lots of enemy prisoners, mostly Italians but some Germans. As we came near our field they said there were snipers, so we had to have our rifles ready. We reached our field in the afternoon. Lots of Lockheed Hudsons flew in. Two enemy aeroplanes flew over. The ground is so hard that we cannot dig a fox hole – there are large stones under the ground.'

If anything, the sand storms in Libya were even worse than the ones that blasted the 57th FG in western Egypt. Sgt Thomas Tackett, a radio technician in the 64th FS, had this recollection;

'I got caught in a sudden and vicious sand storm on my way to the mess tent. I probably wouldn't be here today had I not stumbled into

As supplies of P-40Fs began to dwindle, the Ninth Air Force began getting Allison-powered P-40Ks, identifiable by the extended dorsal fin and the air scoop on top of the nose, as replacements in late 1942. This brightly marked 'No 13' of the 64th FS was assigned to crew chief Frank Roldan in December 1942 and flown by numerous squadron pilots (*W T Robison via Steven Robison*)

one of our fighters, hopped on a wing, climbed into the cockpit, pulled the canopy shut and waited out the storm.'

The mission undertaken on 8 December was typical of the period. Twelve P-40Ks of the 64th FS (three flown by pilots of the newly arrived 85th FS/79th FG) were assigned to bomb the enemy airfield at Marble Arch, Libya, with top cover provided by 12 more Warhawks from the 65th FS.

The P-40K, which was new to the unit, was an Allison-powered version of the Warhawk that had begun arriving in November to replace the 57th FG's ageing and depleted ranks of P-40Fs. Performance of the two models was roughly similar, although the new P-40K was considered slightly faster at low levels. However, its engine only provided full power up to about 15,000 ft, while the Merlin-powered P-40F's operational ceiling was about 5000 ft higher. The 57th FG was the only USAAF unit to fly P-40Ks in the MTO, operating them through the spring of 1943 until more Merlin-powered Warhawks became available. As far as can be determined, only the 64th and 66th FSs flew P-40Ks, while the 65th FS maintained a full complement of P-40Fs.

The formation, led by Capt Richard E Ryan of the 64th FS in P-40K 'No 20', approached the target at an altitude of 5500 ft under an overcast sky. Several Bf 109s were seen taking off from the airfield a few minutes before the P-40s released their bombs, and these enemy fighters made an aggressive attack as soon as they reached sufficient altitude. Capt Ryan got a shot at one of them on the first pass and claimed the aircraft as damaged. Claims of two aircraft destroyed apiece were confirmed for 1Lt George Mobbs and 2Lt Steven Merena of the 64th FS, plus 1Lt Arnold Jaqua of the 65th FS. One further victory went to 1Lt William S Barnes of the 64th FS. Despite his two scores, this was a tough mission for 1Lt Mobbs, who recalled;

'I was flying P-40K "No 11" on that mission. I had gotten good shots at two different Me 109s during the fight. Because of the intensity of the fight I hadn't observed the final results of the first one (which Merena confirmed). The second one was in a downward spiral, and I tried to watch it down. This lack of caution led to my problem. Suddenly, holes appeared in my left wing. It seemed to take a long time for me to realise

1Lt George Mobbs of the 64th FS barely made it back to his base for a belly landing in P-40K 'No 11' following a difficult mission on 8 December 1942. After downing two Bf 109s, Mobbs was shot up by several others and only just missed being wounded by a shot that ripped through the fuselage (*Lyle Custer*)

what was happening. I started a tight turn and moved into a position to retaliate, but when I pulled the trigger nothing happened. My guns wouldn't fire. I also realised I was now alone.

'I started trying to make headway toward our lines, hoping to get to friendly territory in case I had to go down. It was difficult to make progress. As soon as I would head toward home I was attacked. I then observed that there were two above, two on my left and two above to my right. Two from one side would make a pass and I would turn into them, and then the two from the other side would make a pass. In an attempt to make better progress I thought I would turn into them only to the point that I could see the cannon hole in the Me 109's nose spinner – maybe then they wouldn't be leading me enough, and I could make more progress toward home. Somewhere in here I took a hit in the left fuselage and a fragment in my left thigh.

'Although I have a clear recollection of the thoughts I had as to how to thwart their efforts to shoot me down, the sequence of those efforts is vague in my memory. I know that somewhere in there I thought my chances were so slim that when turning into them I contemplated trying to ram one of the enemy fighters.

'I felt that the German anti-aircraft helped me in my plight because in shooting at me they were also getting close to the Me 109s. Eventually they broke off, either because they were out of ammunition or low on fuel, or both. I made it back to our strip and belly-landed – a very rough belly landing. My trim tabs were ineffective, probably damaged by gunfire, and I was exhausted.

'If you look closely at the Me 109 you will note that there is a hole in the spinner for the cannon. There is also a protrusion (sand filter) on the left side of the engine cowling about the size of an old-fashioned stovepipe. These are two images that I saw frequently in my dreams after that day.'

George Mobbs continued to fly in the 64th FS through to August 1943, scoring four confirmed victories and achieving the rank of major.

Little more than a month after this engagement the 57th FG passed the Marble Arch, which was Mussolini's monument to himself on the

The 8th Army passed the Marble Arch in Libya in December 1942, just in time for a graffiti artist to tag the structure at Christmas! Italian dictator Benito Mussolini had the monument to himself erected on the Via Balbia – the coastal road between the provinces of Tripolitania and Cyrenaica – to celebrate early Italian victories. It was destroyed in 1970 on the orders of Libyan leader Muammar Gaddafi (*Dan and Melinda Shobe*)

border of Cyrenaica and Tripolitania, on the way to its next airfield. In the three months following the 8th Army's breakout at El Alamein, Montgomery's troops chased the *Afrika Korps* some 1400 miles across Egypt and Libya. With the capture of Tripoli on 23 January 1943, Montgomery paused to regroup and replenish his forces. Ahead of him in southern Tunisia stood the Mareth Line, Rommel's seemingly impenetrable defensive position running from the Gulf of Gabes to the Dahar and Matmata Hills to the west. Beyond the hills lay the barren wastes of the Dahar and the Grand Erg Oriental sand desert.

Built by the French prior to the war to protect its Tunisian colony from the Italians in Libya, the Mareth Line consisted of steel and concrete fortifications and an underground communications system. When Rommel's forces reached the line in late January, the respite allowed by Montgomery gave the *Afrika Korps* time to add tank traps, minefields, gun emplacements and miles of barbed wire. Luftwaffe fighters of JG 77 were stationed close behind the line on airfields at Zuara, Bir Toual, Gabes and El Hamma. Any frontal assault on the Mareth Line was bound to be a costly, bloody affair.

On 23 December 1942, Maj Art
Salisbury assumed command of
the 57th FG from Lt Col Mears.
Salisbury, formerly CO of the
65th FS, is shown here behind
the steering wheel of his Jeep
as he talks to some of his pilots.
He commanded the group until
April 1944, flying 128 missions
before transferring to England as
commander of the Ninth Air Force's
84th Fighter Wing (*Art Salisbury*)

Pilots were not the only 57th FG
personnel in harm's way during the
desert campaign. In addition to the
threat of air raids on their landing
grounds, enlisted men could get hurt
during road convoys. On the last day
of 1942, Pvts Robert Holland of the
64th FS and Robert Berkey of the
66th FS hit a mine with their
ammunition truck as they
approached an overnight bivouac
area in the Libyan desert.
Fortunately, both men survived
the blast, and their cargo did not

detonate (*Lou Lederman*)

Armourers of the 65th FS bore-sight P-40F 'No 53' on a desert landing ground, likely Hamraiet. On 20 January 1943, Lt Richard Kimball damaged a Bf 109 while flying this Warhawk near Gorina. Sadly, this was the mission in which Capt Marshall Sneed of the 65th FS was shot down and killed (*Bob Hanning via www.57thfightergroup.org*)

The 57th FG was by this time a fully functioning, efficient fighter-bomber unit of the DAF. Ninth Air Force, recognising the outstanding job Frank Mears had done in commanding the 57th FG during its formative period, promoted him to wing headquarters. Maj Art Salisbury, 65th FS CO, replaced Mears as group commander on 23 December 1942, and he would lead the 57th for more than a year before he too was tapped for a bigger job.

Much of the credit for the progress made by the group must go to the hard working and dedicated groundcrews.

February 1943 was a relatively quiet time for the USAAF fighter squadrons in Libya, as most of the aerial action involved Twelfth Air Force aircraft over Tunisia in connection with Rommel's thrust through the Kasserine Pass. In March, the DAF began in earnest the process of softening up the Mareth Line. It was on one of these missions that 1Lt Edward H 'Duke' Ellington of the 65th FS had a frightening, but memorable, experience. He recounted;

'We were on the deck strafing in the Medinine area when my P-40 took a 20 mm round in the wing, which resulted in a huge hole. I broke for the coast and stayed on the deck until I was certain I was behind friendly lines. When I cut in I was well behind our own landing strip and came upon a British P-40 re-supply unit.

'When I landed the RAF sergeant took a look at my bird and said, "Damn, Yank. You've got a problem there". I can't remember his exact words, but the paraphrase is pretty close. The aeroplane was gushing fuel from its ruptured tanks, and you might say that I had a lucky day since I was damned fortunate not to have run out of fuel over the sea. The amusing thing about this incident was that the sergeant then said, "Yank, do you want another aeroplane?" I hadn't realised that this was a re-supply outfit, but naturally I was eager to get back to my strip. So I jumped at the chance, even though this aeroplane's cockpit was configured for British use and was somewhat different from ours.

'By now it had been several hours since I had left my revetment at my home strip. They all knew I was missing. My appearance, taxiing into my own revetment with a new aeroplane after taking off on a mission in my old one, was hard to explain'.

One of the original pilots who had flown off the *Ranger*, Ellington extended his combat tour in the 65th FS and flew 116 missions before

The three victory markers below the cockpit of Lt Roy Whittaker's 65th FS P-40F 'No 43' *Miss Fury* date this photograph as having been taken after 11 January 1943, when he was credited with a confirmed victory during a scrap with Bf 109s near Barat. Note the aeroplane's name applied to one of the cowling panels stored under the wing. The rudder marking signified A Flight of the 65th FS (*Bob Hanning via www.57thfightergroup.org*)

being sent home in September 1943. He returned to the 65th FS in November 1944 and was promoted to squadron CO shortly after the war ended. He flew 180 combat missions in World War 2 and stayed in the USAF until 1968, when he retired with the rank of colonel.

On 13 March 1943, the 57th FG experienced its most spirited engagement with enemy fighters in many weeks. The mission was a fighter sweep to the Gabes area, with 36 P-40s of all three squadrons participating. Several of the pilots flying in the 64th FS were members of the newly arrived 324th FG, the third American P-40 unit assigned to the DAF. Pilots of the 314th FS/324th FG had been assigned to the 57th FG to gain experience.

The formation flew from the 57th FG's base at Ben Gardane out over the sea, and then turned in across the coastline just north of Gabes. Heavy anti-aircraft fire bracketed the 64th FS, which was flying at low altitude. Then the formation was attacked by Bf 109s, and a huge dogfight erupted. One of the P-40s was hit immediately and it dove out of the formation towards the shoreline but was not seen to land. This was probably Capt John Simpson, a flight leader in the 314th FS who was flying his first combat mission and was taken prisoner, spending the rest of the war in captivity. Two pilots of the 66th FS, which was flying top cover, recorded their memories of this battle. First, 2Lt John E Teichrow, who flew P-40 'No 75' that day;

'On my 22nd mission, 13 March 1943, our squadron was attacked by approximately 25 Me 109s. The total flight lasted about 1 hr 45 min and was a typical free-for-all melee. I recall firing instinctively at a Me 109 as he flew in front of me, and I was surprised to see pieces of his rudder and elevator flying off. He never saw me – I couldn't hit the side of a barn with a handful of sand.'

1Lt Dale Deniston, flying P-40 'No 27', recorded the same day's action in his diary;

'What a terrific day. Only training flights in the morning. I took a wonderful bath and had a change to clean clothes. At 1400 hrs we went out on a fighter sweep to the Gabes area. The 64th FS led with 12 aircraft, followed by the 65th FS with 12 aircraft as middle cover and the 66th FS providing top cover. I was in tip top cover in Jim Curl's section, him leading. I led the element, with Charlie Leaf as my

Lt Edward 'Duke' Ellington of the 65th FS sustained serious damage to his P-40F 'No 61' during the assault on Rommel's Mareth Line in March 1943. When his aeroplane took a nasty hit in the starboard wingtip from ground fire, Ellington turned out to sea and then flew east to reach friendly territory. The tough P-40 held together, and Ellington made an emergency landing next to a British re-supply unit (*Edward Ellington*)

wingman. Near Gabes, at 18,000 ft, we were attacked by 15+ Me 109s and Macchi 202s.

'God! What a fight followed. I got in a fair firing burst. Lost from my formation, I flew all over the place – aeroplanes swirling thick as flies. I saw one hit the water below. We have four pilots missing, none from our squadron. It was the longest and fiercest fight I've ever been in. Lasted at least 20 minutes. Maj Worley of the 314th shot down but is safe.'

Lts Teichrow and Deniston were each credited with one Bf 109 damaged. Confirmed victories were awarded to 1Lt William S 'Tommy' Beck of the 64th FS, 1Lts Thomas Boulware, John Gilbertson and Thomas T Williams of the 66th FS and Maj Archie Knight, 57th FG operations officer, who also claimed two Bf 109s damaged but was shot down just behind German lines near the beach. Knight managed to evade the enemy until nightfall, then took to the water and by swimming and wading made his way to the British lines. Also shot down were two pilots of the 64th FS, Lts Robert Douglas, who was taken prisoner, and William E Jenks, killed in action.

Fondouk fell to American troops on 28 March, and the 8th Army passed Gabes three days later. Although Axis forces were again in retreat, the fighting was far from over in Tunisia. It would take the combined forces of Montgomery and Eisenhower another two months to achieve total victory in North Africa. During that period, the Warhawk units of the Ninth Air Force would continue to pound away at ground targets, and to take on the Luftwaffe and *Regia Aeronautica* at every opportunity.

In the early afternoon of 2 April 1943, Capt Lyman Middleditch of the 64th FS/57th FG led eight P-40Ks out of Soltane landing ground for an armed reconnaissance mission covering the coastal highway along the Gulf of Gabes. As the formation crossed the bomb line at

P-40K 'No 34' of the 64th FS was aptly named, as the limited altitude capability of the Allison-powered fighters usually forced their pilots to wait for their adversaries in high-flying Bf 109s to attack from above before engaging them. Lt William Jenks, the regular pilot of *MESSERSCHMITT BAIT*, was killed in action on 13 March 1943, although he was flying a different P-40 at the time (*Lyle Custer*)

10,000 ft, Middleditch, flying P-40K 'No 11', spotted 20+ Bf 109s flying northward from the Gabes area. Obviously, the German pilots had seen the P-40s as well, as they climbed slightly then turned left into the sun and dove from 11,000 ft at the American fighters.

Capt Middleditch had been watching the Bf 109s all the time, and he was not surprised by the attack. He turned his formation into the diving fighters, and soon the sky became a mass of swirling aeroplanes. As was often the case in these circumstances, pilots from both sides were so busily engaged in looking for targets while avoiding their opponents that they found it difficult to get off a shot. On this occasion Capt Middleditch was the only P-40 pilot who had a chance to open fire, pumping 300 rounds into a passing Bf 109. Then, as quickly as the engagement began, it was over. Middleditch reformed his eight P-40s and led them back toward their base, dodging a barrage of heavy flak on the way. Later, Middleditch described the fight that made him an ace;

'We spotted some 20+ Me 109s, which came in to attack, rather hesitantly, I thought. Things didn't look too good at first, but their hesitation gave us time to get set. They probably thought we were baiting them with a small formation, since we'd had things so much our way during the past few days.

'After a few minutes of manoeuvring one of the Jerries made a pass at me. He was a little late in pulling out. I saw my tracers go into his wing root and some pieces flew off the right wing. Then I noticed a few "golf balls" float by my prop and knew that some of Jerry's friends were on my tail. I quit my victim and went into a spin to evade. It worked, but I missed the opportunity to see the aeroplane I'd hit go into the deck. The ground forces later confirmed the crash.'

However, Capt Middleditch initially did not claim the Bf 109 he hit as being destroyed because the 64th FS sortie report lists enemy casualties of just one Bf 109 damaged. Apparently the claim was upgraded to a confirmed destroyed when later evidence came in. Be that as it may, the Ninth Air Force acknowledged its first ace six days after the scrap, crediting Middleditch with five victories. The 28-year-old New Yorker completed his combat tour in July 1943 and returned to the US, where he spent the rest of the war in Training Command.

'PALM SUNDAY MASSACRE'

Of all the missions flown by P-40s in the MTO, none stands out so clearly as the 57th FG's late afternoon show of 18 April 1943, known by the participating pilots as the 'Goose Shoot', but soon upgraded by the press corps to the monicker 'Palm Sunday Massacre'. On that single mission, Warhawk pilots of the 64th, 65th and 66th FSs and the 314th FS/324th FG (a recent arrival in-theatre) were credited with destroying no fewer than 74 German aircraft during a 20-minute engagement over the Gulf of Tunis, losing just six of their own. In addition, four pilots joined the Ninth Air Force's list of aces that day.

It should come as no surprise that such a lopsided victory took place in the closing days of the Tunisian campaign. As the Axis forces squeezed tighter and tighter into the Cape Bon area, it became clear to them that their cause was lost. For several weeks before Palm Sunday, large formations of Luftwaffe transport aeroplanes had been shuttling back and forth between Cape Bon and Sicily.

Initially, the primary purpose of the flights was to carry reinforcements and war material to North Africa, and later they began evacuating troops. Considering the air superiority enjoyed by the Allies over Tunisia, it was just a matter of time before the shuttle flights began to run into trouble. In encounters on 10 and 11 April at Cape Bon, P-38 Lightnings of the Twelfth Air Force had downed no fewer than 50 Ju 52/3m tri-motor transports. It was also reported that USAAF B-25 bombers on a shipping sweep over the Mediterranean had shot down a number of Ju 52/3ms with their turret guns.

From dawn on 18 April 1943, intelligence reports reaching the 57th FG headquarters at El Djem indicated that the Germans were planning a big airlift of key personnel from Tunis to Sicily. Col Art Salisbury, CO of the 57th FG, duly began sending out patrol missions during the day, but time after time they returned to base with nothing to report. With hope of a big score fading, Col Salisbury laid on the final mission of the day in coordination with No 244 Wing RAF. Some 48 P-40s from his four squadrons, with a top cover of No 92 Sqn Spitfires, took off for a maximum effort patrol just before dusk. The Warhawks began departing El Djem at 1705 hrs under the leadership of Capt James G 'Big Jim' Curl, a highly experienced flight leader of the 66th FS.

Capt Curl led the Warhawks northward, with his 66th FS in low position and the others stacked up to the 64th FS on top. Two P-40s

As the Allied advance into Tunisia gained ground in April 1943, the Luftwaffe began flying mass missions to and from Sicily with Ju 52/3m transports to evacuate key *Afrika Korps* personnel and equipment. On 18 April, the 57th FG caught a huge formation of these aircraft off Cape Bon and decimated it in the famous mission that the press nicknamed the 'Palm Sunday Massacre' (*Francis Hudlow via www.57thfightergroup.org*)

dropped out with engine trouble and returned to base. After picking up the Spitfires for tip-top cover, the remaining 46 P-40s skirted the coast from Sousse to Nabual. Then Curl turned northwest and crossed Cape Bon, before heading out over the Gulf of Tunis under an overcast sky.

With the light beginning to fade, Curl turned the formation around and headed south from about six miles offshore. Then, as if by magic, there appeared before him a huge formation of tri-motored transport aeroplanes flying in a 'V-of-Vs' formation low over the water. There was no time to count them, but he later estimated seeing close to 100 aeroplanes below him. Curl glanced back over his shoulder to ensure the Spitfire escorts were in place, then ordered the Warhawks to attack.

Curl's squadron, at the bottom of the formation, and the 314th FS, in low cover position, were closest to the transports and made first contact. The medium cover 65th FS followed them in, but the 64th FS and the Spitfires above were attacked by Bf 109s that were escorting the transports. Capt Curl described his view of the engagement for a Ninth Air Force publication;

'When I first saw the Jerry aeroplanes they were right beneath us, about 4000 ft down. Camouflaged as they were with green colouring,

The P-40F assigned to Col Art Salisbury in the spring of 1943, 'No 01 '(41-14235) was maintained by personnel of the 66th FS. Later transferred to the 65th FS, the fighter was shot down during a ground attack mission on 6 November 1943 near Metkovic, Yugoslavia, Lt Robert Blackshaw being posted missing in action (*Bob Hanning via www.57thfightergroup.org*)

Capt Jim Curl, a highly experienced flight leader in the 66th FS nicknamed 'Big Jim', led the Palm Sunday mission in P-40F 'No 92' *Buckeye Blitz*. He scored three victories during the engagement and went on to command the squadron from May through to August 1943. He was killed in action flying P-51s later in the war (*New England Air Museum*)

it was rather difficult to distinguish the transports against the sea. When we got near they looked like a huge gaggle of geese, for they were traveling in perfect "V" formation, tightly packed. The boys simply cut loose and shot the daylights out of them. What concerned our pilots most was the danger of hitting our own aircraft, for the concentration of fire was terrific and the air was filled with whistling and turning machines. There were cases of pilots missing the transport they aimed at and hitting the one behind. It was as fantastic as that – you just could not miss.

'There was no real fighter opposition because the British Spitfires that were flying our top cover did a grand job in keeping the Messerschmitts so busy that they could not interfere with our attack to any extent.'

Capt Curl was credited with two Ju 52/3ms and one Bf 109 destroyed, plus two tri-motor transports damaged. Promoted to major and given command of the 66th FS shortly thereafter, he completed his first combat tour in August 1943 and returned to the US. He came back to the MTO in late 1944 to command a Mustang squadron in the 52nd FG but was killed in action on 19 March 1945.

Three pilots attained the unusual status of 'ace in a day' on 18 April by destroying five aircraft. One of them, 2Lt Arthur B 'A B' Cleaveland of the 66th FS, got five Ju 52/3ms but was so excited when he got back to El Djem that he dug in the wingtip of his P-40 on landing and wrecked the aeroplane. The other two were members of the 314th FS.

Capt Roy Whittaker, by now a highly experienced flight leader in the 65th FS, already had three victories to his credit, and added four more on 18 April. He recalled the fight for a reporter;

'I attacked the Ju 52s from astern at high speed and fired at two aeroplanes in the leading formation. The bursts were short and the only effect I saw was pieces flying off the cabin of the second ship. I pulled away and circled to the right and made my second attack. I fired two bursts into two more Ju 52s – again in the leading formation. They both burst into flames. The second flew a little distance and then crashed into the water. I lost sight of the first and didn't see it hit. I then made a third pass and sent a good burst into the left of the formation, at

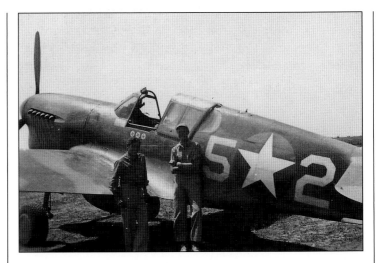

A very pleased Lt Harry Stanford and his crew chief pose with their 65th FS P-40F 'No 52' shortly after the Palm Sunday mission, in which Stanford was credited with three Ju 52/3ms destroyed. It is likely that the two-colour camouflage on this short-fuselage Warhawk was applied during an overhaul at the maintenance depot in El Kabrit, Egypt (*New England Air Museum*)

another Junkers. As I pulled away, it crashed into the water. By that time the Me 109s were among us. As I pulled up to the left, I saw a Me 109 dive through an element of four Warhawks, and I tagged on his underside and gave him a long burst in the belly. He crashed into the sea from 1000 ft.

'I then joined up with some Warhawks that were lufberrying with six Me 109s. I met one of these fighters with a quartering attack and hit him with a short burst. Pieces flew from the aeroplane and he started smoking, but climbed out of the fight. It was a pilot's dream. I'd never seen such a complete massacre of the enemy in my life. I was afraid someone would wake me up'.

Whittaker's four victories brought his total to seven, making him the top-scoring pilot in the 57th FG. It was an honour he would retain throughout the war. At the time, he also stood as the top ace of the Ninth Air Force. Returning to the US in June 1943, Whittaker became a flight instructor for the US Military Academy at West Point and ended the war as a major. He remained in military service, seeing combat in the Korean War and finally retiring with the rank of colonel in 1973.

Unlike Whittaker, 2Lt Richard O Hunziker, of the 65th FS was a rookie pilot. On only his second combat mission of the war, 2Lt Hunziker was flying P-40F 'No 61' as wingman for his squadron commander, Maj Gordon F Thomas. Hunziker, who would finish his combat tour in 1945 as group operations officer, contributed this account in the book *Desert Campaign*, an official publication of the Ninth Air Force;

'The enemy formation looked like a thousand black beetles crawling over the water. I was flying wing ship on Maj Thomas, who was leading our squadron. On our first pass I was so excited I started firing early. I could see the shots kicking up the water. Then they hit the tail section of a Ju 52 and crawled up the fuselage. This aeroplane was near the front of the first "V". As I went after it I realised I was being shot at from transports on both sides. It looked as though they were blinking red flashlights at me from the windows – Tommyguns, probably. The ship I was firing at hit the water with a great sheet of spray and then exploded.

Maj Gordon Thomas, CO of the 65th FS, admires the rudder art of *'Rouge'* on his P-40F. Thomas led the squadron from late December 1942, when he took over from Art Salisbury, until he was reassigned back to the US in May 1943. Note the extended trim tab on the rudder (*Bob Hanning via www.57thfightergroup.org*)

As I pulled up I could see figures struggling away from what was left of the aeroplane.

'I'd lost Maj Thomas. There were so many P-40s diving, climbing and attacking that it was difficult to keep out of the way of your own aeroplanes. I made a circle and then heard someone say over the radio "There's Me 109s up here – come up and help us", so I climbed to 5000 ft and flubbed around among the dogfights, not knowing just what to do. Finally I got on the tail of a Me 109. As I was closing I noticed flaming red golf balls streaming past me on both sides. That meant there was another enemy fighter directly behind me, firing with his 20 mm cannon.

'So I took evasive action. That brought me over the shoreline, where I hooked onto another enemy fighter. My first squirt hit near the nose of the Messerschmitt. Pieces flew off, and he went into a steep dive. I followed him closely, still firing, until he crashed in a green field with a big splash of smoke and flame. Then I heard them giving instructions to reform.'

Another replacement pilot from the 65th FS to taste success on the mission was 2Lt Alfred Froning, who shot down two Ju 52/3ms. He would subsequently 'make ace' in December 1943 while flying P-47 Thunderbolts with the squadron.

The 64th FS provided extremely effective top cover for the other squadrons, knocking down six Bf 109s for no loss to themselves. One of the top-cover pilots was 1Lt R J 'Rocky' Byrne, who would reach ace status a week later. Here is his report, given shortly after landing from the mission;

'The MEs were all messed up. I got three of them, but that isn't anything. I had a ringside seat for the whole show. All you could see were those big ships coming apart in the air, plunging into the sea and crashing in flames on the beach. Their fighters couldn't get in to bother our ball carriers at all.'

The final kill tally for the mission was as follows – 64th FS, six Bf 109s and 0.5 of a Ju 52/3m; 65th FS, three Bf 109s, two Bf 110s (although German sources state there were no examples of Messerschmitt's twin-engined fighter destroyers in the area at that time) and 12 Ju 52/3ms;

66th FS, three Bf 109s and 23.5 Ju 52/3ms; and the 314th FS, two Bf 109s and 22 Ju 52/3ms. In addition, Lt Col W K 'Sandy' McNown, CO of the 324th FG, was also credited with two Ju 52/3ms destroyed.

The Warhawk pilots had administered a stunning blow to the Luftwaffe, so it was not surprising that the German bombers pounded the field at El Djem on the night of 19 and 20 April in retaliation. Sadly, 1Lt Alan H Smith, a highly decorated 64th FS pilot who had scored 1.5 victories in the 'Goose Shoot', was killed by a bomb fragment, and seven other men were injured. Four P-40s were also destroyed in the raids.

The losses at El Djem, although painful, were inconsequential to the big picture in Tunisia, however. The Warhawk squadrons duly continued with their relentless pounding of the now demoralised Axis forces on Cape Bon.

The 64th FS added the final two names to its list of aces on 26 April, when 2Lts R J 'Rocky' Byrne, flying P-40K 'No 37', and R J 'Jay' Overcash, in his P-40K 'No 13', destroyed two Bf 109s apiece while escorting RAF Baltimore bombers. Some 20+ Bf 109s had attacked the formation over the target, and the squadron's mission report gave this account of the action;

'2Lt Byrne got on an Me 109's tail and gave it a burst. The Me 109 started down and then turned back up, and 2Lt Byrne gave him a second good burst. Immediately following, 2Lt Byrne attacked another Me 109. Flt Off Marcum saw the Me 109 at which 2Lt Byrne had been shooting in flames and going toward the deck. Flt Off Marcum

Col Art Salisbury, at extreme right, reads letters of congratulation received from Gen George C Marshall, US Army chief of staff, and others to the 57th FG pilots who participated in the Palm Sunday mission. To his great frustration, Salisbury missed the mission because he had flown earlier in the day (*Art Salisbury*)

duly claims an Me 109 destroyed for 2Lt Byrne. 2Lt Byrne continued after his second Me 109, got in two good bursts and saw the enemy aeroplane go over on its back and the engine explode. 2Lt Byrne claims a destroyed enemy aeroplane. 2Lt Byrne got in some shots at a third Me 109 but makes no claim from that engagement.

'2Lt R J Overcash spotted a pair of Me 109s coming across just above himself and Capt Mobbs. Then six Me 109s came in from "three o'clock", and 2Lt Overcash got in a long burst on the leading enemy aeroplane. It started down toward the deck but turned back up, so 2Lt Overcash went down and got in a good 30-degree deflection shot on the enemy aeroplane. The Me 109 started for the deck trailing smoke. When the enemy aeroplane was at 2000 ft 2Lt Overcash was engaged by another Me 109. He turned back up, spun out and upon recovering saw the Me 109, which he had been following, crashed and burning on the deck. 2Lt Overcash claims an Me 109 destroyed.

On 26 April 1943, with the North Africa campaign drawing to a close, 2Lt R J 'Rocky' Byrne of the 64th FS reached his goal of becoming an ace when he destroyed two Bf 109s on an escort mission for his fifth and sixth confirmed victories. Another 64th FS pilot, 2Lt R J 'Jay' Overcash, also made ace during the mission (*Carl Lovick*)

'Lt Overcash then formed up with four friendly aircraft and started home. Just prior to crossing the bomb line area, two Me 109s attacked from "nine o'clock". Lt Overcash got a good shot at the leading enemy aeroplane, saw it roll over on its back and explode, going toward the deck in flames. Lt Overcash claims a second 109 destroyed.'

The victories brought Byrne's total to six and Overcash's to five. Both men would soon complete their tours and return home, where they left the service at the end of the war. They were recalled to active duty during the Korean War, and Overcash, who had a career in the textile industry, went on to help design the uniforms for the newly established Air Force Academy in 1954.

On 12 May 1943, with the vaunted *Afrika Korps* now surrounded and thoroughly beaten, General von Arnim surrendered and the long battle for control of North Africa came to a close. The men of the 57th FG briefly celebrated their victory, then prepared for whatever was to come next. The 57th FG had flown 350 missions – 4730 sorties – and claimed 130 confirmed aerial victories (group headquarters two kills, 64th FS 41.5, 65th FS 36 and the 66th FS 50.5) during the North Africa campaign. Of the 72 pilots who had flown their P-40s off the *Ranger* some ten months before, five were dead and four more were prisoners of war.

This period map shows the multitude of airfields and landing grounds occupied by the 57th FG from El Alamein through to VE Day

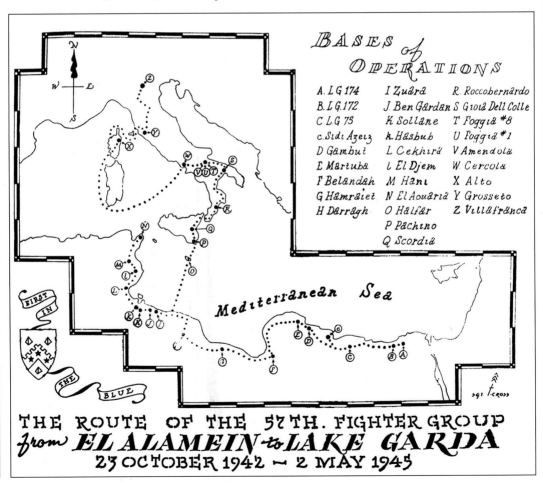

BASES of OPERATIONS

A. L G 174   I Zuára   R. Roccobernárdo
B. L G. 172   J. Ben Gárdán   S Gioia Dell Colle
C L G 75   K Sollâne   T Foggiá #8
c. Sidi Azeiz   k. Hâshub   U Foggiá #1
D Gámbut   L Cekhirá   V Amendola
E Mártubá   l El Djem   W. Cercola
F Belándáh   M Háni   X Alto
G Hámráiet   N El Aouáriá   Y Grosseto
H Dárrágh   O Hálfár   Z Villáfránca
                    P Páchino
                    Q Scordiá

THE ROUTE OF THE 57TH. FIGHTER GROUP
from EL ALAMEIN *to* LAKE GARDA
23 OCTOBER 1942 ~ 2 MAY 1945

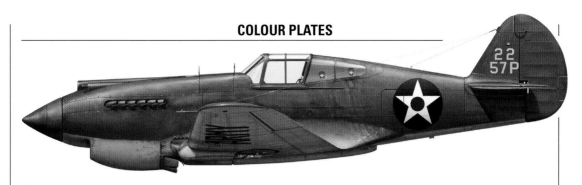

1
P-40B (serial unknown) of the 64th PS, Day Field, Windsor Locks, Connecticut, USA, August 1941

2
P-40E 41-5726 of Capt Philip G Cochran, 65th FS CO, East Hartford, Connecticut, USA, April 1942

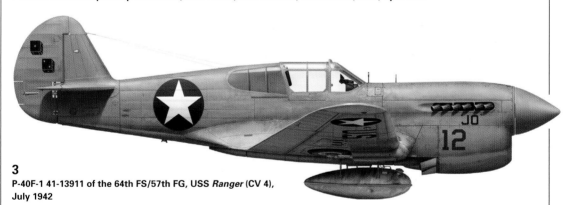

3
P-40F-1 41-13911 of the 64th FS/57th FG, USS *Ranger* (CV 4),
July 1942

4
P-40F-1 41-13878 of 2Lt Thomas T Williams, 66th FS, LG 97, Egypt, 4 September 1942

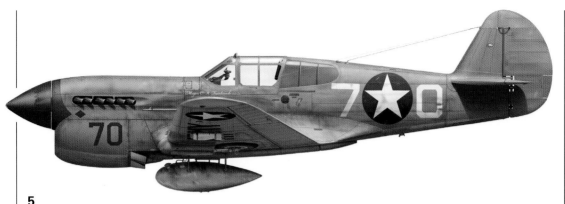

5
P-40F-1 (serial unknown) of Maj Charles R Fairlamb, 66th FS CO, Maryut, Egypt, September 1942

6
P-40F-1 (serial unknown) *Miss FURY!* **of 1Lt Roy E Whittaker, 65th FS, LG 174, Egypt, October 1942**

7
P-40F-1 (serial unknown) *The Shadow* **of 2Lt A Wade Claxton, 66th FS, Martuba, Libya, November 1942**

8
P-40F-1 (serial unknown) *???/Heil Heel* **of the 66th FS, Belandah No 2, Libya, December 1942**

9
P-40F-1 (serial unknown) *UNC A BUD* of Capt Marshall Sneed, 65th FS, Bir Dufani, Libya, 20 January 1943

10
SM.79 (serial unknown) of 2Lt William P Benedict, 66th FS/57th FG, Darragh West, Libya,
February 1942

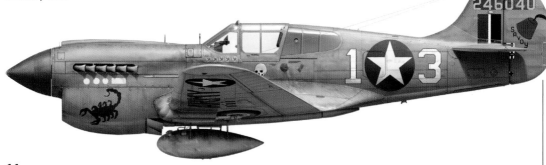

11
P-40K-1 42-46040 of Capt R J 'Jay' Overcash, 64th FS, Tunisia, May 1943

12
P-40F-20 41-20019 of Capt Dale R Deniston, 66th FS, Gozo, Malta, July 1943

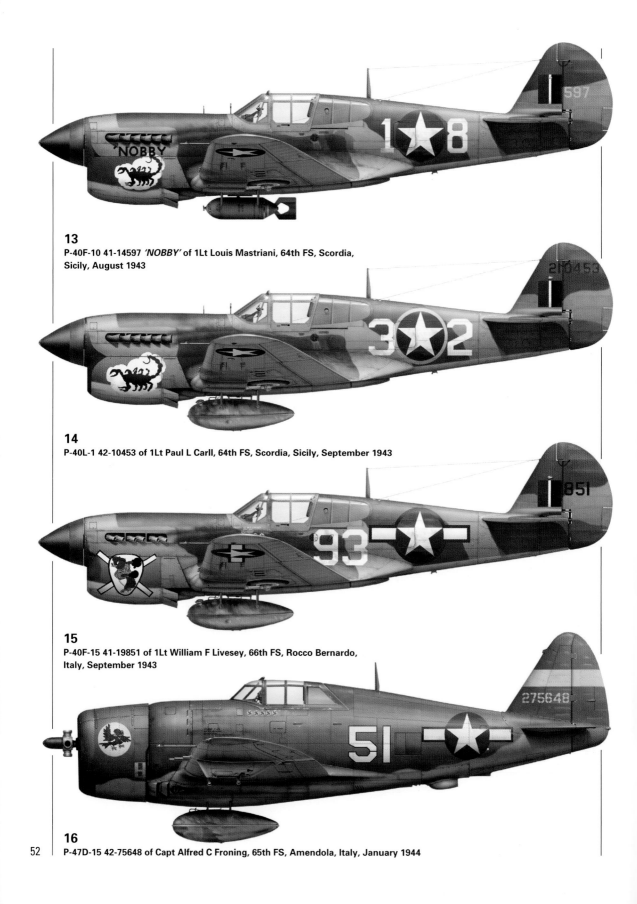

13
P-40F-10 41-14597 *'NOBBY'* of 1Lt Louis Mastriani, 64th FS, Scordia,
Sicily, August 1943

14
P-40L-1 42-10453 of 1Lt Paul L Carll, 64th FS, Scordia, Sicily, September 1943

15
P-40F-15 41-19851 of 1Lt William F Livesey, 66th FS, Rocco Bernardo,
Italy, September 1943

16
P-47D-15 42-75648 of Capt Alfred C Froning, 65th FS, Amendola, Italy, January 1944

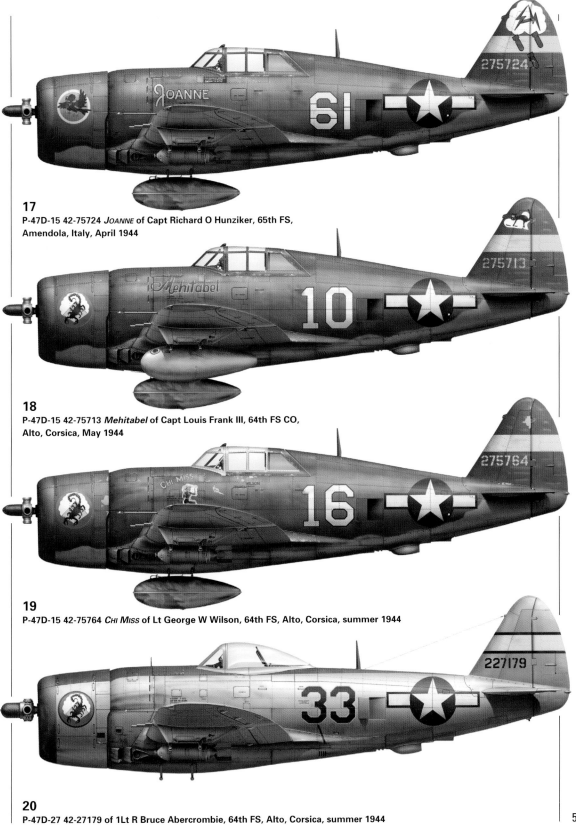

17
P-47D-15 42-75724 *JOANNE* of Capt Richard O Hunziker, 65th FS,
Amendola, Italy, April 1944

18
P-47D-15 42-75713 *Mehitabel* of Capt Louis Frank III, 64th FS CO,
Alto, Corsica, May 1944

19
P-47D-15 42-75764 *CHI MISS* of Lt George W Wilson, 64th FS, Alto, Corsica, summer 1944

20
P-47D-27 42-27179 of 1Lt R Bruce Abercrombie, 64th FS, Alto, Corsica, summer 1944

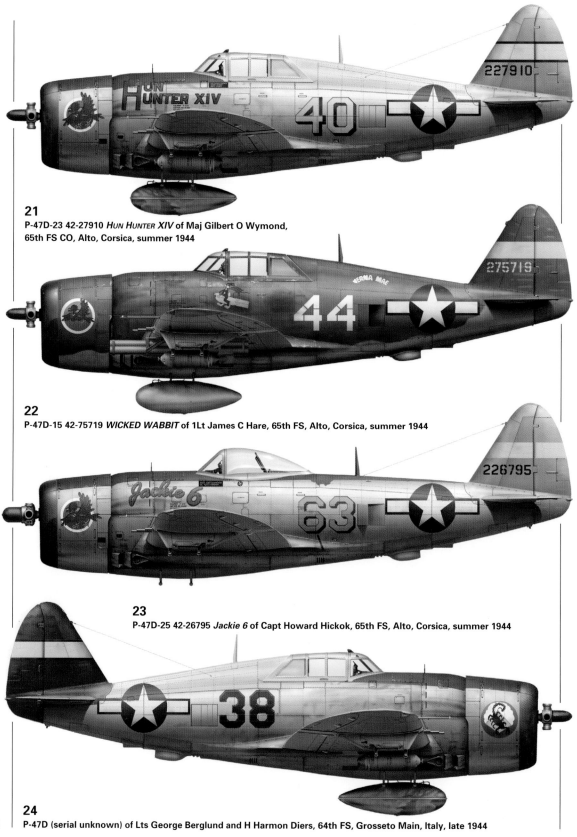

21
P-47D-23 42-27910 *Hun Hunter XIV* of Maj Gilbert O Wymond,
65th FS CO, Alto, Corsica, summer 1944

22
P-47D-15 42-75719 *WICKED WABBIT* of 1Lt James C Hare, 65th FS, Alto, Corsica, summer 1944

23
P-47D-25 42-26795 *Jackie 6* of Capt Howard Hickok, 65th FS, Alto, Corsica, summer 1944

24
P-47D (serial unknown) of Lts George Berglund and H Harmon Diers, 64th FS, Grosseto Main, Italy, late 1944

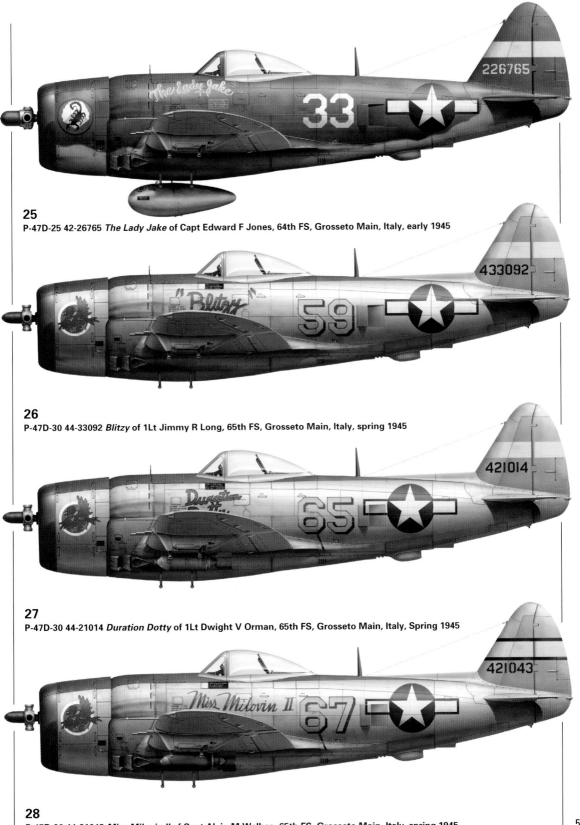

25
P-47D-25 42-26765 *The Lady Jake* of Capt Edward F Jones, 64th FS, Grosseto Main, Italy, early 1945

26
P-47D-30 44-33092 *Blitzy* of 1Lt Jimmy R Long, 65th FS, Grosseto Main, Italy, spring 1945

27
P-47D-30 44-21014 *Duration Dotty* of 1Lt Dwight V Orman, 65th FS, Grosseto Main, Italy, Spring 1945

28
P-47D-30 44-21043 *Miss Milovin II* of Capt Alvin M Welbes, 65th FS, Grosseto Main, Italy, spring 1945

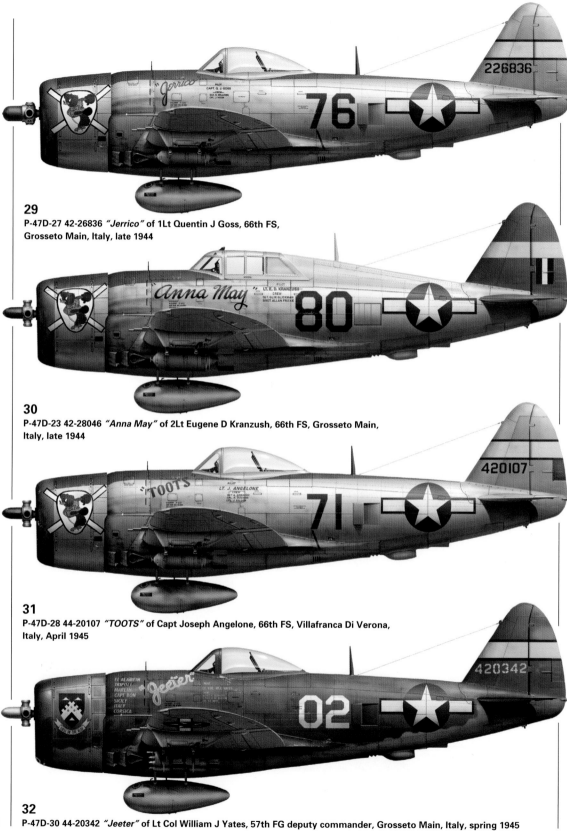

29
P-47D-27 42-26836 *"Jerrico"* of 1Lt Quentin J Goss, 66th FS,
Grosseto Main, Italy, late 1944

30
P-47D-23 42-28046 *"Anna May"* of 2Lt Eugene D Kranzush, 66th FS, Grosseto Main,
Italy, late 1944

31
P-47D-28 44-20107 *"TOOTS"* of Capt Joseph Angelone, 66th FS, Villafranca Di Verona,
Italy, April 1945

32
P-47D-30 44-20342 *"Jeeter"* of Lt Col William J Yates, 57th FG deputy commander, Grosseto Main, Italy, spring 1945

1
57th FG

2
64th FS

3
65th FS

4
66th FS

1

2

3

INVASION FORCE

With the capture of North Africa complete, the 57th FG had several weeks to relax and regroup before the next phase of the air war in the Mediterranean began. The group's air echelon moved to a landing ground at El Haoaria, on Cape Bon. Rumours circulated among the enlisted ranks that the entire group would be sent back to the US to assist in training new combat units, but time would prove these rumours to be as unreliable as most. Still, many of the remaining pilots from the *Ranger* deployment – including such notables as top ace Roy Whittaker and the commanders of the 65th FS and 66th FS, Gordon Thomas and 'Jeeter' Yates, respectively – were indeed sent home to pass on their hard-earned knowledge of air combat to pilots in training.

Several veteran pilots who had missed out on the Palm Sunday mission were allowed to extend their combat tours. Art Salisbury continued to command the group. Glade 'Buck' Bilby retained command of the 64th FS and Gil Wymond assumed command of the 65th FS. Remarkably, Wymond would subsequently remain as CO of his squadron for the rest of the war, minus a short leave he took in 1944 to get married. In the 66th FS, Palm Sunday leader 'Big Jim' Curl took over.

The extended fuselage of the late-build P-40F and P-40L is plain to see here as two 64th FS Warhawks fly in formation during the summer of 1943. Lt George Blednick is at the controls of 'No 20', while Lt Paul Carll is flying P-40L-1 'No 32' 42-10453 (*Bruce Abercrombie*)

It was also during this time that the Allison-powered P-40Ks in the 64th and 66th began to be replaced by both new long-tailed P-40Fs and P-40Ls. The 65th FS had retained P-40Fs throughout the North African campaign, but the 64th was fully equipped with P-40Ks after December 1942, and the 66th flew a mixed collection of both types. The new Merlin-powered Warhawks featured slightly better altitude performance and improved directional stability. Some of the low-time P-40Ks were subsquently ferried all the way to China, where Gen Claire Chennault's Fourteenth Air Force was chronically short of combat aircraft.

Prior to the end of the fighting in Tunisia, Allied brass had begun looking ahead to the invasion of Sicily as a preliminary step in the campaign to capture Italy. Before the attack on Sicily could begin, however, the Mediterranean islands of Pantelleria and Lampedusa would need to be wrested from the Italians. Strategically located between Tunisia and Sicily, the islands would present a threat to the invasion force if left in enemy hands. Pantelleria, in particular, featured an airfield with underground hangars built into a hillside. It also bristled with coastal artillery.

Not wishing to expend time and resources on a water-borne invasion of the islands unless absolutely necessary, the Allies decided to first try to subdue them with a massive aerial assault. Units of the DAF, including the 57th FG, and the Twelfth Air Force, were combined under a single command for the effort, which commenced on 18 May 1943.

Allied fighters had a number of spirited combats over Pantelleria during the campaign, but the pilots of the 57th FG did not get into the fight until early June, so it missed most of them. The group's first two victories came on 7 June when a formation of 12 P-40s from the 65th FS on a fighter sweep and reconnaissance mission scrapped with enemy fighters. The leader, Capt Wymond, flying the group CO's Warhawk 'No 01', damaged a C.202, while single victories over Bf 109s were credited to Lt Henry Barker in P-40 'No 57' and Lt James Hadnot in P-40 'No 59'.

The group's only other Pantelleria victories came on 11 June when, during a morning mission, Lts Charles C Leaf and Louis R Bigelow of the 66th FS shared in the destruction of a Bf 109G five miles west of Pantelleria. About an hour later, the 64th FS sent 16 P-40s toward the island. Flying one of the Warhawks was 2Lt William F Nuding Jr, a replacement pilot on just his ninth mission. He described his experience in a letter to the author;

'I was flying "tail-end Charlie" when I spotted three Bf 109s making a head-on pass at my flight. I called the squadron leader and met the lead fighter head on, shooting the right-side engine cowl completely off the aeroplane, with further hits to the right side of the fuselage and continuing out the right wing as I broke left to avert a collision. I then turned sharp right into the two remaining Bf 109s. Pulling enough lead until the second aircraft was completely hidden under the nose of my Warhawk, I opened fire, with the Bf 109 coming into view within seconds and continued to fire on down to zero deflection. I noted many hits from the nose of the Bf 109 back down the right side of the

2Lt William F Nuding Jr (second from left), who was a 64th FS replacement pilot flying just his ninth mission, scored his first victory over Pantelleria on 11 June 1943. He is shown here with the groundcrew of his Warhawk 'No 28' *Ruthie*. These men are (from left to right), Orrin Shipp, Rade Chuich and Joseph Felix (*Orrin Shipp*)

fuselage, shattering the cockpit glass. I could clearly see these hits from a distance of only a few hundred feet.

'At this time I noticed the third Bf 109 off my left wing going into a tight left turn, pulling streamers. Not wanting him on my tail, I broke left and locked onto him. My first burst hit him on the left side. The aeroplane made an abrupt pull-up to the vertical and fell off into a spin and on into a vertical dive, with me in pursuit. The spin stopped, so I fired a long burst into the Bf 109. By this time it was losing coolant (white smoke) and a brownish substance. We were both in the dive when my guns quit firing, out of ammunition. It also occurred to me that the Bf 109 and I were extremely close to the water. I immediately went into a max G-force pullout, just missing the water.

'By now I was close to a small naval task force heading for Pantelleria. Looking up, I saw four aircraft with round wingtips. From my position they looked like C.202s. Being out of ammo, I headed for a US Navy cruiser and began circling it. The round-wingtip aeroplanes turned out to be P-39s escorting the task force. They had observed my Bf 109 encounter and later confirmed the last kill. That was the only one of the three I received credit for shooting down. I left the area and returned to Cape Bon.'

It was unfortunate for Nuding that he did not receive victory credits for the first two Bf 109s as those, plus two others scored later in his combat tour, would have given him a total of five confirmed destroyed, elevating him to the 57th's roster of aces.

TO SICILY

The surrender of Pantelleria on 12 June was a victory for air power, and it cleared the way for the invasion of Sicily, code named Operation *Husky*. An advance party of the 57th FG moved to Malta, where the Warhawks flew bombing missions in support of the invasion, which began on 10 July. Meanwhile, B Group parties from the squadrons were at Causeway, in Tunisia, preparing for the move to Sicily. Ground personnel and equipment moved by ship to Sicily and reunited with the advance party at a captured Luftwaffe airfield south of Catania. The pace of operations picked up considerably as the P-40s pounded the retreating enemy forces on the northern end of the island.

On Sicily, pilots and groundcrew alike shared in the dangers of combat. Luftwaffe night raiders attacked the airfield several times, although fortunately the damage was limited to loss of sleep as opposed to loss of life. In the air, the group commander and two of his squadron commanders went down in the first two weeks of *Husky*.

Col Art Salisbury, commanding officer of the 57th FG, was shot up by flak over Sicily on 25 July 1943 but managed to nurse his damaged P-40 back to friendly territory before bailing out. He was picked up by British troops and returned to his unit, which he continued to command until January 1944. Note that Salisbury's P-40 was decorated with the badges of all three squadrons, the 64th, 65th and 66th FSs (*Carl Lovick via www.57thfightergroup.org*)

Capt Gil Wymond of the 65th FS was on a strafing mission when he flew through the debris thrown into the air by an exploding ammunition truck. The radiator in the nose of his P-40 was punctured and the engine soon failed due to overheating. By this time Wymond had crossed back into friendly territory, and he was able to make a successful forced landing near Syracuse. Then Col Art Salisbury took a flak hit on 25 July while strafing about 35 miles behind enemy lines. He coaxed his crippled P-40 up to about 2000 ft during a tense five-minute flight toward safety before bailing out near Agira, where he was picked up by British troops.

Major Buck Bilby of the 64th FS had an even more traumatic experience two days later, when the engine in his P-40 failed while he was flying off the east coast of Sicily. He bailed out into the sea and drifted in his inflatable dinghy for more than 24 hours before an air-sea rescue (ASR) launch picked him up. That was the end of combat for Bilby – he was on his way home two weeks later, replaced as 64th FS commander by 1Lt Art Exon.

The Luftwaffe withdrew its fighter units to the Italian mainland at the end of July, but the 64th FS had one more scrap with Bf 109s over Sicily on the last day of the month. Now flying from the airfield at Scordia, Capt Gerald Brandon was leading nine bomb-carrying Warhawks on an anti-shipping patrol in the Malazzo area with a top cover of six Spitfires when the formation spotted six Messerschmitts and attacked. Lts Exon and Mike McCarthy got good hits on one enemy fighter that dove away trailing smoke, and they were awarded credit for a shared probable. Then 2Lt Bill Nuding put several bursts into

One of the last P-40Ks assigned to the 57th FG, 42-45993 met its end on 27 July 1943 when the engine cut out on take-off from Tripoli while Lt Dick Maloney (in boots holding a bent propeller tip) of the 64th FS was ferrying it to Heliopolis to turn it in. Note the yellow border on the national insignia, the RAF fin flash and the red propeller spinner – all standard markings of the period. Group markings had been removed (*Bruce Abercrombie*)

a Bf 109 that was attacking his wingman. The enemy fighter caught on fire and crashed into a mountain near the coast, giving Nuding his second confirmed victory of the summer.

Enemy resistance on Sicily ended on 16 August, and the Allies' attention now turned to the main event – the invasion of Italy. Six days later, the 57th FG was transferred to Twelfth Air Force in preparation for the big event.

ITALY INVADED

The British 8th Army's XIII Corps crossed the Straits of Messina on 3 September 1943 to make an amphibious landing at Calabria, on the toe of Italy. Although the Italian government quickly capitulated, German forces soon figured out that this was not the main thrust of the invasion and withdrew to the Italian boot to prepare for the main landings, which would take place six days later at Salerno and Taranto.

On the first day of the invasion, the 57th FG sent 24 Warhawks from the 64th and 65th FSs to escort B-25s attacking enemy positions at Camigliatello, in Italy. Lt Paul Carll was flying P-40 'No 38' in the 64th FS's Red Section, providing top cover for the mission. He recalled the sortie in a 2003 letter to the author;

'About the time we turned onto a northerly course, I spotted German fighters at about "five o'clock" and coming out of the sun. I was the first one to spot the enemy, and called out to the squadron, "Snappers at 'five o'clock' and closing"'. It took a few seconds for the others to spot them, but we were all were primed for the attack. At a strategic moment I called, "Turn about right" (*text continues on page 68*).

Two P-40s of the 66th FS take off from Scordia, Sicily, in September 1943 for a mission over mainland Italy. Note the radio mast on the closest Warhawk, 'No 79', suggesting it may be one of the rare short-tail P-40L-1-CUs. P-40 'No 75' in the background was assigned to Lt Charlie Leaf (*Bruce Abercrombie*)

SALISBURY'S SCROUNGERS

Scrounging, as any USAAF veteran knows, was an essential military skill during World War 2. Fuelled by the imaginations of men with more time than materials at their disposal, drop tank containers became furniture, gasoline tins were fashioned into stoves and thousands of other items that started as one thing became something else. It was a worldwide phenomenon.

Another level of scrounging existed that might be described politely as the unauthorised transfer of items from one unit to another. In this, as in so many other aspects of military operations, the 57th FG excelled. These activities began soon after the group commenced operations in North Africa, where the fast-moving battle front and large quantities of abandoned enemy equipment and aircraft created opportunities for acquiring all sorts of interesting items. Colourful examples abound – 66th FS crew chief Lou Lederman used a Spandau machine gun from a wrecked Stuka to fire away at low-flying Luftwaffe strafers; the 57th FG operations section converted an Italian

bus into a rolling operations office; a stabiliser off of an abandoned Bf 109 became the top of the 66th FS officers' club bar; and it was a rare pilot who was not hankering to make a flight in a captured German or Italian fighter.

The arrival of two replacement pilots in the 66th FS in January 1943 elevated the game to new heights, however. Lts William P 'Red' Benedict, a former Royal Canadian Air Force (RCAF) pilot, and Charles G Leaf, who had flown in the desert with the RAF, quickly became known as the leading exponents of 'midnight requisitioning' in the MTO. In fact, Benedict arrived at the 57th FG in a Spitfire V assigned to his former unit, fully intending to keep the aeroplane until convinced otherwise by his new group commander.

Benedict and Leaf viewed the combat zone as their own private shopping centre, with no cash required. One of their first acquisitions was an Italian SM.79 bomber in reasonably good condition that they liberated from newly captured Castel Benito airfield. With the help of several enlisted mechanics, they got

Capt Ed Silks, 65th FS intelligence officer, used this Fiat sedan for transportation during 1943.

Possessing intimate knowledge of scrounging techniques gained by experience, Silks painted a large

'Fighting Cocks' squadron badge on the door to clearly establish ownership of the car (*Ed Silks*)

the aeroplane airworthy and refuelled. Although neither pilot had flown a multi-engined aircraft before, they calmly fired up the three motors and flew the bomber back to their base at Darragh, where groundcrewmen quickly painted over its Italian markings with American stars. The 'Green Goose', as the aeroplane came to be known, ferried men, supplies and mail back and forth among desert bases for about a month. No doubt the 'Goose' served as the getaway aeroplane for several Benedict-Leaf capers before she had to be abandoned.

While the 57th was in Sicily, Benedict and Leaf once showed up at Scordia in a B-25 that they hasd'found' in North Africa. The group commander, Col Salisbury, usually turned a blind eye toward such antics, but on this occasion he chewed out the pilots for taking an unnecessary risk because one of the B-25's engines was smoking when they landed. On another occasion, Benedict had to ditch a Bf 109 off Sicily when its engine failed.

But the pair's crowning achievement occurred shortly after the 57th FG moved to Italy in September 1943. At Taranto, they found an abandoned Piaggio P.108 four-engined bomber that they could not live without. Acting quickly, they flew the Italian aeroplane a short distance to the 57th's new base at Gioia del Colle. The airfield's short runway gave them a scare, but they got down without damaging the aeroplane. As with the 'Green Goose', the Piaggio got a quick repaint job, and to repay the groundcrewmen who pitched in to finish the job, Benedict decided to take them for a ride. Unfortunately, the Piaggio's landing gear failed when Benedict brought it in, and the plane did a cartwheel on the runway before lurching to a stop. No one was hurt, but the last flyable Piaggio P.108 in the world was now relegated to the scrap heap.

Perhaps thinking greater responsibility would clam Benedict down, Col Salisbury promoted him to 66th FS commander in December 1943. He served successfully in that position for about six months before being transferred to another fighter-bomber squadron, and shortly thereafter Charlie Leaf assumed command of the 66th. Leaf led the unit with distinction through to the end of the war.

Lt Bill Benedict of the 66th FS 'liberated' this Italian Piaggio P.108B four-engined bomber from an RAF base at Taranto shortly after the 57th FG moved to Italy in September 1943. It got a quick paint job in USAAF markings before Benedict pranged it in a landing accident (*Gerald Schwartz*)

'We turned into the 109s and I found myself meeting one that was after (Lt Gene) Kowalski in a quartering, head-on confrontation. This must have startled the German pilot because he broke to his right and I found myself on his tail. I squeezed off the 0.50-cals and pieces flew off his aeroplane, part of his right wing came off and his fighter went into a spin. I claimed one Bf 109 destroyed. Kowalski went after another Messerschmitt and hit it pretty well, although he could only claim it as damaged.

'Our Red Section staved off the attack. The Bf 109s broke off, and the B-25s went on to their targets uninterrupted. From our point of view the mission was quite successful. All of our P-40s returned to Scordia'.

Unfortunately, Lt Kowalski was killed in a take-off accident just 15 days later.

The 57th FG continued to fly support missions over the invasion front for the next two weeks before moving to Rocco Bernardo, an unfinished landing ground on the Italian mainland, on 18-19 September. Ground personnel and spare pilots crossed the straits in a landing craft, the three-mile trip lasting an hour. The group, along with the 79th FG, was assigned to support the British invasion force pushing north from Taranto. A week later the P-40s moved to Gioia del Colle, a modern airfield near Taranto, and then pushed on to Foggia on 2 October.

By this time all of southern Italy had been captured, but the Allied armies stood facing the Volturno Line, the first of a series of prepared defensive positions running across Italy from which the Germans would fight delaying actions in the hope of containing the Allies south of Rome. The Allied advance in southern Italy duly ground to a halt. Field Marshal Albert Kesselring, commander of the German forces,

The 66th FS ground echelon board the naval vessel LST No 343 at Messina, in Sicily, for the overnight trip to mainland Italy on 16 September 1943. Note that the trucks are being backed into the ship so they will be able to pull forward when they depart at the end of the voyage (*Gerald Schwartz*)

Bombed-up Warhawks of the 65th FS await take-off orders in the autumn of 1943. By this time, the national markings had been adorned with white rectangles on either side of the star, as well as a red border, as seen here. Lt Harold T Monahan would be shot down and killed in the second P-40 in this line-up, 'No 54' *Bernice*, on 20 December 1943 (*Wayne Dodds via Mark O'Boyle*)

using the rugged terrain to his advantage, managed to establish a defensive barrier across the Italian peninsula roughly 80 miles south of Rome. Called the Gustav Line, it stretched from just north of Naples on the west coast to the Trigno River on the east. The 57th FG would spend the rest of 1943 aiding the bloody effort to break through the Gustav Line.

Lt John Teichrow belly-landed P-40F-15 41-19851 'No 93' at Rocco Bernardo, in Italy, after hitting a 64th FS P-40 while taking off for a test flight to slow-time the engine on 18 September 1943. The crew chief of 'No 93', SSgt Lou Lederman, was not pleased (*Bruce Abercrombie*)

Bad weather began to hamper operations over Italy in early October, so Twelfth Air Force aircraft began to venture eastward across the Adriatic Sea to hit targets in Greece, Albania and Yugoslavia. Limited by the range of its P-40s, the 57th FG concentrated on missions along the coast of Yugoslavia, attacking enemy shipping and other targets of opportunity.

On 21 October, ten bomb-carrying P-40s of the 66th FS on an anti-shipping patrol got a bonus when they encountered six Ju 87 Stukas near Vodice, in Yugoslavia, and attacked. Led by Lt William P Benedict, the P-40 pilots destroyed all six of the German dive-bombers without loss. The Warhawks were carrying six 40-lb wing bombs each, and Lt Robert C Schuren attempted to drop his bombs on a Stuka when he ran low on ammunition! He was awarded a shared credit with Lt Cortland McCoy Jr for destroying the Ju 87.

After moving to yet another base – Amendola – on 25 October, the 57th FG would divide its attentions between the Italian mainland and the Yugoslavian coastline for the next four months, flying dive-bombing, strafing, patrol and escort missions. Aerial opposition was beginning to wane at this time, as the Luftwaffe pulled one unit after another out of the Mediterranean theatre to bolster air defences over Germany. But there was no diminution of the danger faced by Twelfth Air Force fighter-bomber pilots as a result. In fact, the concentration and skill of German anti-aircraft defences grew as the war continued. The 65th FS, for example, lost three P-40s over Yugoslavia on 6 November. One of those pilots was remembered fondly by his brother in correspondence with the author. Bob Barker, himself a US Marine Corps combat veteran, wrote;

'My tribute is to 2Lt Henry Hunter Barker Jr. After graduation from high school, Hank enlisted in the RCAF, but then returned to the States when the US entered the war. He was assigned to the 57th FG's 65th FS and flew P-40 Warhawks through North Africa, Sicily and on into Italy.

'His final mission was a raid into the Metkovich, Yugoslavia, area, where there was a high concentration of Gestapo and Nazi build-up. On the third pass over the city, his aircraft was shot down. Local peasants removed his body and buried him in the local graveyard so the Germans never had any knowledge of his remains. Hank was only 23 years old when he was killed on 6 November 1943. Two weeks prior to his death, he found out that he had just become a father.

'Hank knew from an early age of his desire to be an aviator, and in his short life accomplished more than most people do in a lifetime. He was my hero and my brother.'

Although the potential for tragedy was never further away than the next mission, there also were occasions of levity for the pilots and the groundcrews who supported them. Many members of the 65th FS during this period remembered Capt Louis 'Jake' Abraham and his 'No 49' *OLE' MISS*, the P-40 he started flying in July while the squadron was in Sicily. Abraham liked the aeroplane so much that not only did he salute it every time he passed, he also insisted that everyone with him salute, too. 'No 49's' crew chief, Mike Wolniak gave this account of how it started to an Army publicist;

Capt Louis 'Jake' Abraham liked his P-40 'No 49' *OLE' MISS* so much that not only did he salute it every time he passed, but he also insisted that everyone with him salute it too. The 65th FS Warhawk, under the care of crew chief Mike Wolniak, eventually broke the 57th FG's engine endurance record (*John Hunziker*)

'I had just started the engine purring over when Capt Abraham walks up and says, "This is to be my aeroplane, and I guess you're my crew chief. That's a sweet-sounding engine you've got there. What do you say we set a record with her?"'

Wolniak agreed and then saluted. Abraham returned the salute, then turned and saluted the aeroplane. Pretty soon, he had everyone in the squadron doing it. *OLE' MISS* returned the favour. The fighter hauled Abraham on mission after mission, sometimes coming back with battle damage but always coming back. By the time Abraham completed his combat tour and left Italy near the end of the year, the old Merlin in 'No 49' had 148 hours of combat flying on it. One day not long afterward, Wolniak was ushered out of his tent to find the entire squadron lined up at attention. Maj Gil Wymond, 65th FS commander, duly pinned a home-made medal on Wolniak in honour of the fact that *OLE' MISS* had just broken the 57th FG's engine endurance record.

A 64th FS armament crew loads a double-bomb package under the belly of a squadron P-40. Armourers used innovation and sheer will to adapt available ordnance to attachment points on their aircraft. Note a drop tank previously mounted on the P-40 is lying in the background at right (*New England Air Museum via Mark O'Boyle*)

Bob Resconsin, a 64th FS electrician, recalled another occasion when the squadron personnel again resorted to humour to help break the tension of daily operations;

'Just one of the funny happenings was when we had about enough of Spam for chow. One of the men wrote a letter to Hormel asking if they couldn't improve the taste any. Hormel replied that they had NEVER sold any Spam to the Army. So the cooks opened all the Spam cases they could find and piled all the cans in to a mountain of Spam and sent a picture of it to Hormel with "Red" Barret, one of our cooks, sitting

TSgt Herb Gluckman, a flight chief in the 66th FS, hitches a ride to the flightline on a trailer loaded with 500-lb bombs (*Herb Gluckman*)

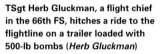

on top. Hormel replied again that we must have been given a shipment meant for the Navy!'

Herb Gluckman, a 66th FS flight chief and one of the earliest assigned members of the squadron, explained to the author how the groundcrews operated;

'Each squadron was divided into three flights – A, B and C – with a flight chief responsible for the mechanical maintenance of the eight aeroplanes in his flight. A crew chief and assistant crew chief were permanently assigned to each ship. A flight chief oversaw the work of his 16 mechanics and made sure the routine inspections were performed as close to periodic schedule as possible, and he frequently had to juggle those schedules because of the squadron's need for aeroplanes to fly missions. However, we did have the authority to ground a ship if we felt that maintenance was being stretched to the point that pilot safety might become an issue. We couldn't pull rank like that too often though.

'Essentially, the responsibility of the flight chief was to "keep 'em flying" by plotting aircraft availability, and this often involved his interceding, on behalf of a crew chief, with a specialty section of the squadron service staff when severe technical problems arose such as when a ship came back shot up, arranging for sheet-metal men to appear. Or arranging to move an aeroplane to our engineering section for an engine or wing change due to combat damage, during which time the chief would reassign the "aeroplaneless" crew to temporarily help the boys of another ship who were overloaded with work. We met with armourers, radiomen etc., to coordinate their needs with the down-times we were scheduling for individual aeroplanes. We frequently rolled up our sleeves and pitched in with the "grease monkey" work, either because the

Capt Bob Hanning, who was the 65th FS's aircraft maintenance officer, poses with P-40F 'No 63'. The aeroplane, assigned to Lt Robert Sherbondy, carried typical markings for late 1943, with red-bordered national insignia, red propeller spinner, thin black outlines on the fuselage numbers and a white disc behind 'Uncle Bud' on the squadron badge. The name *Miss MIAMI* appeared on both sides of the nose (*Bob Hanning via www.57thfightergroup.org*)

Loaded with twin bombs on their centreline racks, P-40s of the 64th FS are lined up for a mission at Amendola, in Italy. The closest Warhawk, with an Indian brave's head painted on the hubcap of its main landing gear, appears to have been fitted with several replacement cowling panels. The third aircraft is Lt Lou Mastriani's 'No 18' *NOBBY* (*Carl Lovick*)

aeroplane's crew was stumped by a problem or to help rush the work along so as to meet the squadron's mission schedules.

'And, of course, the flight chief had to always keep an eye on the squadron's need of his aeroplanes so as to be able to fulfill upcoming mission requirements – how many aircraft were needed, when and did they need to be configured for a long-range mission? If so, he had to make sure belly tanks were hung on the aeroplanes assigned for that mission. We also had to know how many missions were scheduled for the day, and with how many aeroplanes, thus determining which crews to put the pressure on. And with all that, a wise flight chief would also attempt to build and maintain a sense of *esprit de corps* within his small group for the purpose of developing a smooth-running and effective unit. Generally, the compact group of 17 or 18 men (some, mere boys) did work smoothly together, and voluntarily helped each other when needed.

'As far as the working hours were concerned, it was simple – sun-up to sundown, seven days a week, no holidays or overtime. And that pertained to everyone. We had no hangars in which to do our maintenance, nor lighting facilities with which to perform work after dark, therefore all work had to be done during daylight hours. Of course, we wouldn't have used lights even if we had had them. We got enough nighttime visits from uninvited guests as it was without pinpointing our location for them.'

ENTER THE THUNDERBOLT

By the autumn of 1943, time was catching up with the old P-40. The last Merlin-powered Warhawk, P-40L-20 42-11129, had rolled off the Curtiss assembly line in April 1943, and the USAAF did not consider the newer Allison-powered P-40N suitable for combat against the Luftwaffe. But production of the big Republic P-47 Thunderbolt, which showed great potential as a fighter-bomber, was shifting into high gear. In November 1943 the 57th FG began its gradual transition to the radial-engined fighter.

Born of a USAAC specification issued in June 1940 for a heavily armed, 400-mph fighter aircraft capable of high-altitude operation, the P-47 Thunderbolt was a product of Republic Aviation Corporation and specifically its brilliant chief designer, Alexander Kartveli. The P-47 delivered on every count. The aeroplane, designed around a turbo-supercharged Pratt & Whitney R-2800 radial engine delivering 2000 hp, was a massive beast weighing nearly 10,000 lbs empty – about half again the weight of a P-40 – and boasting a top speed of around 425 mph. It was the first American fighter fitted with a four-blade propeller, and its eight wing-mounted 0.50-cal machine guns gave it awesome firepower.

The P-47 first saw combat in Europe in the late spring of 1943 when it undertook bomber escort missions from bases in England with the Eighth Air Force. USAAF pilots, although initially sceptical of the Thunderbolt's ability to match up with contemporary Luftwaffe aircraft, soon came to appreciate its ease of handling, its dazzling performance in a dive and its high rate of roll. Just as important, the fighter's air-cooled engine and robust airframe made it a very difficult machine to shoot down. Once the initial bugs were worked out and the P-47's range was extended with the use of external drop tanks, Eighth Air Force fighter pilots began running up impressive scores in aerial combat. By the end of the war, Republic had manufactured no fewer than 15,660 P-47s – the largest production run of any fighter aircraft in American history.

The Thunderbolt era began in the 57th FG when veteran 64th FS pilots John Patterson, Ed Liebing, Bill Nuding and Lou Mastriani

New Republic P-47D Thunderbolts are delivered by barge to the Twelfth Air Force. The 57th and 325th FGs were the first two groups in the MTO to get the new fighters, conversions beginning in late November 1943. While the 325th used its P-47s primarily on long-range bomber escort missions, the 57th FG developed its Thunderbolts into outstanding fighter-bombers (*New England Air Museum via Mark O'Boyle*)

Capt Bill Benedict, scrounger extraordinaire, assumed command of the 66th FS in December 1943, and the following month the USAAF sent noted artist Maj Charles Baskerville to Amendola to paint a portrait of the colourful pilot. Benedict is seated next to one of his many acquisitions – a trailer he used as both an office and quarters (*Herbert Arnold*)

flew four of the new aeroplanes in from Tunis to Amendola on 28 November 1943 to begin transition training. Mastriani had this to say in a letter he wrote to the author in 2000;

'We were very happy to be re-equipped with the P-47. We had heard a lot of good things about this aeroplane – its speed, durability and firepower. I was one of the first selected to be checked out in the P-47. We flew them back to our squadron and checked out the other pilots.' Mastriani completed 92 missions – the last two in P-47s – during a year of flying with the 64th FS before returning to the US in March 1944.

The transition went slowly as operations continued, weather permitting, in the group's P-40s. 64th FS pilot Bruce Abercrombie recorded in his diary that he did not make his P-47 checkout flight until the afternoon of 14 December. 'Found it a pretty nice ship', he wrote. It would take another month for the 64th FS to complete its transition to Thunderbolts, and the other two squadrons followed shortly thereafter.

The 57th FG could not boast of flying the first P-47 mission in the MTO, as the 325th FG took its new Thunderbolts on an uneventful escort mission to Greece on 14 December 1943 to claim that honour. But the 57th FG did claim the first P-47 aerial victories in the theatre two days later to add this feat to its list of 'First in the Blue' accomplishments.

The 57th FG sent out two overlapping missions on the morning of 16 December. One was a sweep of the Peljasec Peninsula, in Yugoslavia, involving eight P-47s flown by pilots of all three squadrons. Shortly before that mission departed Amendola, 12 P-40s of the 66th FS had taken off for an armed reconnaissance of the Dalmatian coast. The two formations would meet up on the far side of the Adriatic, though not by plan.

The P-47 formation reached its target area in good order and let down to 1000 ft to strafe several small towns on the peninsula. Three pilots of the 65th FS – Lts Al Froning, Robert Monahan and Stan Lancaster – made up Red Section and were trailing the other five Thunderbolts. The group operations report described what happened next;

'Lt Monahan engaged one Me 109 which, at that time, was carrying a bomb and heading west at 1000 ft. Lt Monahan entered a dive, and as combat started the two (aircraft) pulled up to the left, allowing Lt Monahan to get in a long burst at the Me 109. The enemy aircraft began to smoke and then hit the water.

'Lt Froning saw an Me 109 on Lt Monahan's tail during the dogfight and got on its tail. Lt Froning fired and saw pieces fly off the enemy aircraft and the aeroplane crash into the water. He then engaged another Me 109 that had entered the area and received a 20 mm hit in the right wing which started a fire, causing the right wheel to drop down. The fire quickly went out. The Me 109, plus two more German fighters, then got on Lt Froning's tail and were firing at his aircraft from a line abreast formation. In a three-minute battle, his aircraft was badly damaged in the fuselage, and it was also shot through the prop.

'Lt Froning managed to evade two of the enemy aircraft and led the third past a P-40, thereby distracting the Me 109 and managing to get

Capt Al Froning of the 65th FS, his crew chief Don Williams (right) and his unnamed armourer pose with their P-47D-15 42-75648 'No 51' shortly after Froning shot down two Bf 109s over Yugoslavia on 16 December 1943 to become the last ace of the 57th FG. Froning's five victory markers appear below the cockpit, although none of his kills were claimed in this aeroplane (*Mike Williams*)

The changing of the guard from P-40s to P-47s took place at Amendola from December 1943 through to January 1944. Here, P-40F-20 41-20010 'No 10', assigned to 64th FS commander Capt Art Exon, awaits its next bombing mission while groundcrews work on a new P-47 in the background to prepare it for combat (*W T Robison via Steven Robison*)

onto its tail. He got in good bursts on the Me 109 and saw a three-foot section of the wingtip and parts of the tail fall off. The Me 109 was trailing black and white smoke in a 60-degree dive 150 ft from the water when Lt Froning was forced to divert his attention to another enemy aircraft. Lt Lancaster saw the Me 109 hit the water.

'Lt Monahan engaged a second Me 109 following his earlier fight and got in good bursts at 1500 ft before being distracted by another enemy aircraft. He looked back and saw the pilot of the Me 109 that he had hit parachute and the aeroplane crash on the coast.

'Lt Lancaster engaged in a running fight with an Me 109 and followed as the enemy aircraft climbed vertically from the deck to 7000 ft, both aircraft stalling out at that altitude. He was unable to continue the fight and started toward home.'

The P-40s encountered by Lt Froning were from the 66th FS mission. They managed to join the Red Section dogfight and downed two more Bf 109s, victory credits going to Lts Gerard Meacham and Joseph Reynolds. The two leading P-47 sections did not engage, and all five P-47s returned safely to Italy. One 66th FS P-40 was shot up and its pilot, Lt Bell, was wounded.

The group's Thunderbolts had another encounter with Bf 109s the following day. A mixed formation of seven P-47s and six P-40s took off from Amendola at 1400 hrs on an armed reconnaissance of roads in Yugoslavia. The P-40s and three P-47s of the 66th FS made up the assault flight, with two 65th FS Thunderbolts as medium cover and two more from the 64th FS as top cover. As the formation approached Metklovic at 9000 ft, five Bf 109s were spotted 1000 ft above, heading southwest. The group operations report described the encounter;

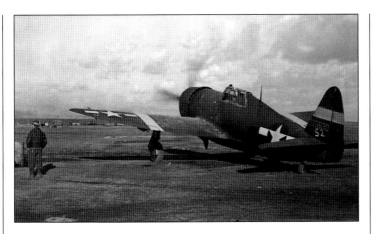

A new P-47D-15 of the 65th FS taxis at Amendola. The aeroplane displays yellow bands around the wings and tail. Along with a red propeller spinner and band around the front of the engine cowling, this would be the standard 57th FG markings for the rest of the war. Although the fuselage number has not yet been painted on 42-75630, it appears that 'No 52' has been hastily applied to the fin (*Bob Hanning via www.57thfightergroup.org*)

'The P-47s immediately attacked the enemy aircraft, and Lt (Ed) Liebing (64th FS) blew the tail of one Me 109 off, causing it to spin in. Lts (Charlie) Leaf and (Hugh) Barlow (66th FS) shared another one, which was seen to crash after the pilot bailed out. The remaining enemy aircraft headed north on the deck, and no further contact was made.'

On the return trip, Capt Carlton Chamberlain of the 64th FS was flying at low altitude in low cloud when his P-47 'No 14' crashed into the sea about a mile off the Italian coast at Manfredonia. He was seen to swim away from the aeroplane, and several boats put out, headed his way. Fortunately, Chamberlain was fished out of the water, and he returned to duty on 24 December.

Christmas Eve 1943 was also the date of the last aerial victory credited to P-40s of the 57th FG. Again, the target was on the far side of the Adriatic, as 12 Warhawks of the 66th FS set out to strafe Preko Harbour on Uljan Island. The sections had spread out in line-abreast formation at low altitude to get under a cloud deck when several of the pilots called in a 200-ft motor vessel in the harbour. The flight leader did not see the ship and could not be reached by radio, so there was no attack. A few moments later, the formation encountered a lone Ju 88 flying east about 15 miles from Sibenik. Walt Henson remembered it vividly, as bad luck deprived him of an almost certain kill;

'We were flying about 5000 ft or so beneath an overcast, and it was dark and dreary at our altitude, but when the sun broke through the Adriatic was glistening and a Ju 88 was silhouetted against the water. We went into about a 15-degree chasing dive with throttles firewalled. He spotted us at "six o'clock". He was right on the water, and black smoke poured out the engines, leaving a wake behind him as the pilot poured the coal to his old kite. I believe it was Charlie Leaf (actually Lt Bob Schuren) who went after him first, but was firing out of range. I was next and got off one or two rounds when my guns jammed.

'The Ju 88 was "S-ing" madly. I was dead astern and not more than 20 ft from it. I could see the tail gunner clearly, reared back in his seat, a little guy wearing a black leather helmet. His face was ashen white and wide-eyed looking up at me. He looked like a 16-year-old kid who was probably terrified. By the time I looked back, "Mac" (Lt Cortland McCoy) had closed in and started firing. The Ju 88 hit the water.'

CHAPTER THREE

Credit for the victory was awarded jointly to Lts Schuren, flying P-40 'No 83', and McCoy, in 'No 85'.

25 December 1943 saw three more missions sent off to Yugoslavia in the morning. The squadrons were released from operations at 1400 hrs to give everyone time to prepare for Christmas dinner two hours later. Later, the bars were open in each squadron's day room, and Col Salisbury made the rounds to offer season's greetings to the men of his command. Bad weather closed in after that, and just one more mission was completed before the end of the year. Then on New Year's Day 1944, a fierce storm blew through Amendola, shredding several tents and soaking the barracks bags and blankets inside. The 66th FS suffered the worst damage, as its cook tent blew down and all the turkeys and pies that were to be served at the noon meal were ruined.

Sunshine returned on 3 January, but no flying was possible at Amendola for another week until the sodden airfield dried out. Tragedy struck on 12 January just as flights were resuming. First, 65th FS pilot Harold Gohman crashed near the airfield while on a test hop in a captured Bf 109. Then Wg Cdr Lance Wade, a 23-victory American fighter ace serving in the RAF, crashed in an Auster III liaison aircraft while taking off after a visit to Col Salisbury and other friends in the 57th FG. Both pilots died.

By this time, the P-40's long tenure in the 57th FG was just about over, and many of the pilots who had flown it in combat were completing their tours. A new generation of replacement pilots was taking their place, including Lt George W Wilson, who soon learned how much his stateside training was valued in the combat zone;

Lt Herman Williams and SSgt Gerald Schwartz of the 66th FS work on their new P-47D-15 42-75833, soon to be 'No 73', at Amendola on 12 January 1944. Williams was shot down by ground fire in another P-47 on 22 February but managed to belly-land the aeroplane on a beach. He returned to duty the following month (*Gerald Schwartz*)

'There were 24 of us pilots trained in P-47 Thunderbolts who went overseas together. We sailed on a liberty ship in a convoy to Oran, North Africa, in November 1943. After ten days there, we were told that we should be at the Fighter Training Center near Constantine. While we were taking showers, after two days and nights on a train, they called off 15 names and said to be ready to leave in half-an-hour, and take your flying equipment. I was one of them. They were taking us to Casablanca, where the P-47s were off-loaded from ships in our convoy. Christmas Day, we stopped in Oran for lunch and then pressed on to Casablanca. There, we test-hopped P-47s, then every day three of us, and a ferry pilot to lead, would take off for the front.

'(Loyst) Towner, (Sheldon) Weber and I were in the last foursome to go. On the way, clouds formed below us and the ferry pilot wasn't sure of our position, so we dropped our external tanks and dived through a hole in the clouds. We saw an airfield and landed – it was an RAF Spitfire base. In landing, Towner blew a tyre and had to stay behind until he received a new one. From there we flew to Tunis for fuel and directions. We then flew to Bari, in Italy, where Weber landed and hit a wire fence. He had to stay there until his aeroplane was checked. The ferry pilot and I finally got to the 57th FG at Amendola.

'We were greeted by Col Art Salisbury, 57th FG CO, who told me I was not going back to Casablanca. When he had learned that 24 P-47 pilots were in the area, he immediately requested that all of us be assigned to the 57th. The orders arrived that day. The others who were ferrying aeroplanes would stay with the group when they arrived with their second aeroplane. I had supper with Col Salisbury and he questioned me about the training etc. that we had had in the States. He told someone to find me a place to sleep that night – it was on a stretcher in an ambulance! The next morning the nine pilots arrived from the training centre, and we were divided among the three squadrons. (Harry) Williams, (Allen) Sanderson and I were assigned to the 64th FS.'

COMMAND CHANGE

On 20 January 1944, Col Art Salisbury addressed his men to let them know he was being sent on temporary duty to England, where his expertise in tactical operations would be helpful in preparing the Ninth Air Force for the upcoming invasion of France. At the time, Salisbury thought he would be returning to the 57th FG, but that turned out not to be the case as he was assigned as a wing commander in the Ninth Air Force. After 18 months and 129 missions in the MTO, Salisbury's days on combat operations were over.

Lt Col Archie Knight moved up from group operations officer to assume command of the 57th FG. Like Salisbury, he had flown off the *Ranger* in July 1942. Remarkably, he would remain on operations for the rest of the war – surely one of the longest combat tours in the history of the USAAF.

The 66th FS flew the group's last P-40 mission of the war on 21 January. Lt Weber, flying just his second mission, was shot down by ground fire but managed to survive and return to Amendola. The squadron's remaining Warhawks were flown out the next morning to

Minor teething problems plagued the first P-47s assigned to the 57th FG. Here, P-47D-4 42-22810 'No 27' of the 64th FS has suffered a tail-wheel collapse. The aircraft, assigned to Lt Allen Sanderson, has been painted with the group marking but does not yet carry the 64th FS 'Black Scorpions' badge on the cowling (*Bruce Abercrombie*)

a depot at Naples, where the pilots swapped them for new P-47Ds and flew back to Amendola in the afternoon. SSgt Gerald Schwartz, a 66th FS crew chief, recorded the work that went into preparing his new aeroplane for combat in several diary entries;

'22 January – This afternoon I got my new P-47, brand new, with just three hours flying time on it! I can see that we will all be reading the tech orders for the new aeroplanes instead of books from home. It now appears that there is more work to be done on these aeroplanes than anybody thought. Lt Williams was here all day helping me with the receiving inspection on aeroplane "No 73", and will help out tomorrow when it is washed down (with gasoline). The tachometer is not working and I'll replace it tomorrow. It is interesting to note that all the pilots are helping the crew chiefs to get these aeroplanes operational and cleaned up.

'29 January – I worked all day on my new aeroplane. Glenn Eipper, our artist, painted my number (73) on it. I got some white paint from him and painted Lt Williams' name on it. Lt Turner flew it today on a test hop and it was okay. The oil cooler still leaks, and I will probably have to change it soon.

'3 February – Remarkably, our new aeroplanes finally flew on a mission. They were bomber escorts for B-25s on an uneventful mission north of Rome.

'22 February – Lt Williams was shot down on the first of two missions this morning while dive-bombing with 500-lb bombs. Lt Wise (who flew my aeroplane) said that Lt Williams' ship was hit by ack-ack and went down in flames. Bad weather this afternoon prevented further flights, so we were released at 1500 hrs and several of us went to a USO show and movie tonight at Manfredonia.

'23 February – My aeroplane flew one dive-bombing mission this morning. I heard that Lt Williams, whose ship was downed in flames yesterday, actually managed to belly land on a Mediterranean beach and is safe!'

The initial encounters with enemy aircraft in December had established the P-47's reputation as a competent air-to-air fighter in the minds of the pilots, but the 65th FS commander, Maj Gil Wymond, thought the new aeroplanes needed some significant modifications to make them better fighter-bombers. He enlisted his chief armourer, TSgt Bill Hahn, in the improvement project. Hahn wrote this recollection;

'12 January, Wednesday, a cold wet night. About 2100 hrs the tent flap opened and Maj Wymond was standing there. TSgt Dixon had been rotated back to the States, and I had been made technical sergeant in charge of armament when the armament officer had been transferred to headquarters. Wymond's first words, "Hahn, this aeroplane is no good for close support. It doesn't carry bombs. It has no bomb toggles".

'The major was correct, as there were three small, difficult tank releases on the floor on the left side of the cockpit. It would be impossible to dive, aim and pull the releases for bombs. Wymond continued, "They want to transfer us to England for high-altitude escort, and I ain't going. You are going to convert this crate into a dive-bomber. Come with me to the aeroplane, and I'll show you what

Maj Gil Wymond, longtime commander of the 65th FS, was the driving force behind the development of the P-47 for fighter-bomber operations. Under his direction, the Thunderbolt was modified to improve dive-bombing and strafing accuracy and to increase its bomb load (*Ed Silks*)

TSgt Bill Hahn, chief of armament in the 65th FS, carried out the P-47 modifications requested by Maj Wymond. Working with a helper, Hahn moved the toggles for the wing bombs and drop tank from the cockpit floor to the instrument panel so pilots would not need to take their eyes off their targets while dropping bombs. Other changes followed (*Ed Silks*)

I want". We sat on the wing and discussed this until after midnight. Next morning we began to convert his aeroplane.

'I chose one helper, Charles Appel, and we began to devise a temporary release. It was a real sorry excuse for a solid release, but we accomplished it in two days. We did this on the prototype by laying a flat steel bar across the three releases and applying a fulcrum to the floor to allow the pilot to release the two wing bombs with one pull. This was not a satisfactory application because the belly tank release could not be used easily.'

Despite its obvious shortcomings, the release performed well when Wymond flew a demonstration for some visiting brass, dropping two unfused 500-lb bombs off the end of the Amendola runway. Then Hahn and Appel went back to work on improving the contraption. Again, Hahn;

'Appel and I devised a method of laying the two wing releases on the floor and connecting them with a cable that ran forward up the firewall and back to the instrument panel. We then added the belly tank release. The pilot only had to lean forward in the cockpit, watch his target and pull the two small toggles on the instrument panel to release all of his bombs. This was duplicated in all squadrons until all Thunderbolts were capable of dive-bombing. It was crude but effective, later being improved by Republic Aviation on subsequent P-47D models.'

Wymond was not finished, however. With Hahn's help, he went on to pioneer the dropping of two 1000-lb wing bombs from the P-47. He also developed better sway braces for the bombs and improved the aeroplane's strafing capability by raising the gunsight four inches so the guns could be mounted in a slightly more depressed position. The P-47 went from Thunderbolt to 'Thunderbomber', thanks to their work. Hahn concluded;

On 23 January 1944, Maj Gil Wymond of the 65th FS became the first P-47 pilot to take off carrying two 1000-lb bombs. His P-47 'No 40' *HUN HUNTER II* is seen here at the head of a line-up of 'Thunderbombers' loaded with the big bombs. Note how the landing gear wheels have flattened under the weight (*Bob Hanning via www.57thfightergroup.org*)

'The shame of this whole episode is that Wymond was never recognised for forcing this development and for taking the risk of dropping the first test bombs. He never gave up interest in perfecting the P-47 as a ground support aircraft. Tragically, Col Wymond was killed in a P-84 Thunderjet accident shortly after the war. I feel he deserves recognition for developing one of the best aerial weapons the Allies had in World War 2 "in-the-field". Indeed, his name should appear in air museums around the country, especially where it pertains to the P-47.'

The opening months of 1944 were a trying time for the Twelfth Air Force. While attempting to support two ground offensives aimed at breaking the stalemate on the Gustav Line – the Anzio landing on 22 January and a direct attack on the centre of the line on 1 February – the Twelfth Air Force was also in the process of losing two fighter

The pilots of the 57th FG immediately appreciated the toughness of their new P-47s, which soon became legendary for their ability to withstand battle damage. Lt E C Brown battered the nose of this 64th FS Thunderbolt when he flew through a Lombardi tree while strafing, but he was able to fly the aeroplane back to base nevertheless (*Bruce Abercrombie*)

Four officers of the 64th FS pose outside their tent cabin. They are, from left to right, Capt Lester A 'Doc' Wall (flight surgeon), and pilots R Bruce Abercrombie, Michael C McCarthy and George W Wilson (*George Wilson*)

groups and a medium bomber group that were transferred to the CBI. Partly as a result of this, the 57th FG moved from Amendola, on the Foggia Plain, back to the Naples area and a base called Cercola in the first week of March. From there the group would fly missions against targets near Rome. The overwater missions to Yugoslavia ended following this move.

57th FG P-47s had three scraps with enemy fighters during the month they were based at Cercola, downing four for the loss of 64th FS pilot Lt Loyst Towner. 66th FS pilot Lt Dave Coughlin was shot down and killed near Rome by a Spitfire on 24 March in a friendly fire incident.

Losses to accidents and ground fire continued as well. Lt Bruce Abercrombie of the 64th FS, who had damaged an Fw 190 on 24 March, had an exciting entry for his diary six days later;

'Today was a big day for me – I finally got it. As we were on our way up to the north of Rome we drew some flak from Gaeta. The first burst hit me, knocking out my supercharger regulator and getting an oil line. This caused my engine to freeze up, and I had to belly-land into the water just off the coast, about three miles from Mount Circeo – 30 miles into "Jerry land". Fortunately though, my wingman, Paul Rawson, stuck around and directed a Walrus ASR aeroplane out to me. I was picked up and deposited at Capodichino. I remained in the hospital until evening and then went back to Cercola.'

On returning to base, Abercrombie learned that the 57th FG had pulled out for reassignment to Corsica. He flew to the island, off the northwest coast of Italy, in the group's B-25 the following day. A new chapter in the story of the 'First in the Blue' 57th FG was about to begin.

OPERATION *STRANGLE*

With the Allied armies stalled south of Rome in the spring of 1944, the Mediterranean Tactical Air Forces rolled out a new plan to break the stalemate by destroying the supply network that was feeding German forces on the Gustav Line. Dubbed Operation *Strangle*, the tactical air interdiction campaign would target rail, road and waterborne traffic across the narrow waist of Italy. The 57th FG, with its heavy-hitting P-47 'Thunderbombers', was slated to play a major role in the offensive.

Operation *Strangle*, brainchild of Gen J K 'Uncle Joe' Cannon, commander of Mediterranean Tactical Air Forces, opened in mid-March while the 57th FG was still at Cercola. It was the first full-scale, consciously planned interdiction campaign of World War 2. Initial attacks were directed against the Italian rail system, with the goal of forcing the Germans to shift their transportation to the less efficient roads and rivers, which would then be pounded as well. The strategy worked to a certain extent, cutting the enemy's daily supply tonnage significantly. But the transportation system had such capacity in Italy that Operation *Strangle* could not possibly live up to its name.

An unforeseen benefit of the offensive would soon emerge, however, as the aerial assault paralysed the tactical mobility of the German armies just as the Allies began their assault against the heavily fortified enemy positions. Within three weeks, the four-month stalemate on the ground

Initial attacks of Operation *Strangle* were directed against the Italian rail system, with the goal of forcing the Germans to shift their transportation to the less efficient roads and rivers. Once perfected, the P-47s were able to deliver ordnance on specific targets, such as this shattered rail bridge at Castiglione della Pescia, with pinpoint accuracy (*Jim Long*)

had been broken and the German army was in full retreat. The enemy withdrew some 200 miles, suffering an estimated 70,000 casualties – about one-third of its forces in Italy.

On 25 March 1944, the ground personnel of the 57th FG left Naples in a British-crewed liberty ship, bound for the island of Corsica. The men got a spectacular view from Naples harbour of the ash cloud emanating from nearby Mount Vesuvius, which has been erupting for several weeks. The sea was rough for the entire overnight trip north, and many of the men suffered from seasickness. However, as 66th FS crew chief Gerald Schwartz noted, 'If there was any benefit to be derived from being seasick for many guys, it was that they were too sick to care whether or not we were to be bombed or torpedoed!'

The 57th FG disembarked on the afternoon of 26 March at Ejaccia, on Corsica, and the men spent the night at a nearby quartermaster camp. The next morning they embarked on a 170-mile road convoy north to Alto airfield, on the east coast of the island just south of the port city of Bastia. The group's P-47s flew in from Italy on 30 March and commenced operations from Alto the next day.

The 57th FG, as the Twelfth Air Force's only operational P-47 group (the 79th FG was still transitioning from P-40s at this time), was charged with operating as a separate task force from Corsica across the Tyrrhenian Sea to strike deep behind the enemy's right flank. Its designated targets were the rail network and communications links, with the destruction of locomotives, rolling stock and motor vehicles as the top priority. Although the group was directed to fly a minimum of 48 sorties per day, it achieved an average of 80 per day during the first two weeks of operations, and improved from there when the weather permitted.

A flight of four P-47s from the 64th FS had just strafed a train south of Florence on 6 April when the leader, Capt Lou Frank III, spotted a fighter pilot's dream – ten Italian BR.20s and one SM.79 flying southeasterly at 3500 ft with no fighter escort. As the P-47s attacked,

Engine changes started when the 57th FG's P-47s began to accumulate flying hours. Here, the 65th FS engineering crew has just removed the Pratt & Whitney R2800 from a Thunderbolt and is about to begin stripping the cowling from it (*Bob Hanning via www.57thfightergroup.org*)

the enemy formation split up, with six bombers heading east and five south. The 64th FS combat report described what happened next;

'Capt Frank pulled up behind the group of six and attacked out of the sun. He fired bursts into the left engine of one, setting it on fire. He last saw it at 1000 ft with its nose down, headed for the deck. Maj Carlton A Chamberlain (group operations officer at that time) saw it crash and burn on the ground. Capt Frank then attacked one of the group of five with bursts into the left engine, which caught on fire. He and Lt R K Nevett witnessed one open 'chute from this aircraft and last saw the aeroplane on fire at 600 ft out of control and headed for the deck. Capt Frank and Lt Nevett then chased another enemy aircraft down to 100 ft above the deck. Capt Frank put bursts into the right engine and rear top turret. Lt Nevett's bursts struck across the top of the fuselage near the cockpit. Capt Frank witnessed a piece of the right wing fall off, and he and Lt Nevett claim damage to this aircraft.

'Maj Chamberlain attacked the SM.79 in the group of six. It dived after he fired bursts into the fuselage from a position of direct line astern. He then attacked another aeroplane before returning to the SM.79, putting more bursts into the fuselage, from which pieces tore away. At this time the enemy aircraft was at a height of just 50 ft. Maj Chamberlain claims one damaged enemy aircraft. When it dived down after the first bursts, Maj Chamberlain attacked a BR.20, with bursts into the left side of the fuselage. Pieces fell away and the aeroplane caught fire. One 'chute was seen to open by Maj Chamberlain and Lt John J Lenihan. The aeroplane was headed down out of control. Maj Chamberlain claims this BR.20 destroyed. In this area Frank, Chamberlain and Nevett saw three aircraft burning on the ground.

'Lt Lenihan shot at one enemy aircraft at its extreme left and behind its left engine. He then put a burst into its left side and it caught fire. He last saw it going down in flames out of control and claims it destroyed. He then put bursts into the left side of another enemy aircraft, which immediately caught fire. Lt Lenihan saw it hit the ground in flames and claims this enemy aircraft destroyed. He then proceeded to attack a third enemy aircraft, striking bursts into its left side centre. This aeroplane caught fire, and he last saw it at 300 ft going down in flames out of control. Lt Lenihan claims this enemy aircraft destroyed.'

The score for the mission was six confirmed destroyed and one damaged. All four P-47s returned safely to Alto, although Lt Nevett's 'No 24' had suffered battle damage. Two weeks later, Capt Lou Frank would assume command of the 64th FS after Maj Art Exon was shot down and taken prisoner.

As the pace of operations intensified, so did the risks faced by the pilots. From April 1943, when the USAAF instituted Missing Aircrew Reports (MACRs), up to the 57th FG's move to Corsica at the end of March 1944, the group had filed 20 MACRs. In the coming 13 months through to the end of the war in Europe, the 57th would more than quadruple the number of MACRs filed to 84. The vast majority of missing pilots would be lost to ground fire. While some returned to their squadrons and others were later reported as being prisoners of war, most of the missing pilots were never seen again.

Pilot Al Welbes and his crew chief Roy Richard pose with *'Miss Mi-lovin'*, their well-worn P-47D 'No 67' 42-75972. The significance of the swastika on the cockpit rim is unknown, as Welbes had no aerial combat claims. He flew the aeroplane for most of his tour before it was shot down in March 1945 with Lt Clarence 'Rip' Hewitt at the controls. The latter became a PoW and Welbes got new P-47D 'No 67' 44-21043, which he named *'Miss Mi-lovin' II'* (*Al Welbes*)

Consider the example of 65th FS pilot Al Welbes. He beat the statistics, completing 116 missions and returning home in the spring of 1945 with the rank of captain. Welbes was one of the lucky ones;

'I was in a shipload of replacements that left Camp Patrick Henry in April 1944 and stopped in Oran, where we transferred to a British ship and proceeded to Naples. The trip took ten days, as I recall. I was in a group of eight pilots assigned to the 57th FG, and after a few days in Naples we were picked up by the 57th's B-25 and flown to Corsica. Myself and Richard Coleman, who was later named "King" for the squadron bar, went to the 65th FS. Two others went to the 64th FS and four to the 66th FS. Coleman and I were the only ones of the eight to return home in normal rotation. The six other pilots became PoWs or were killed in action.'

Even veteran pilots like 57th FG operations officer Carlton Chamberlain were not immune to the dangers of operational flying, as he described nearly 50 years after the fact;

'One day when I was taking off on a mission from Corsica, the thrust from my propeller suddenly went to zero. We never found an explanation for it. I was just short of take-off speed, and was probably three-quarters of the way down the runway, when the thrust dropped away. I knew I wasn't going to take off, and I knew I wasn't going to be able to stop before I reached the end of the runway either. Therefore, I knew there was going to be a crash.

'I was carrying a full load of 0.50-cal ammunition and two 500-lb bombs, and I didn't want to be in a fire with all those explosives. I decided to jettison the bombs. I pulled the release, and those two bombs bounced end over end, keeping pace with me all the way down the runway! I had, of course, not armed the bombs, but I still didn't feel much comfort in that, inasmuch as they were bouncing on their fused noses every other cartwheel. They didn't explode, and I sailed off the end of the runway. I had taken every precaution that I could think of like turning off all electrical switches and closing the throttle, etc.

'The area near the end of the runway had been built up so that it was level with the runway, and consequently there was a substantial drop-off past the end. In addition, there was a small creek that ran cross-wise of the direction of the runway. My wheels caught on the far bank of the creek and caused the aeroplane to flip over onto its back.

'Because of the creek, the emergency vehicles had to go a long way to reach the crash. Several guys got there quickly on foot, however, and found me lying beside the inverted P-47 still wearing my parachute. There was only three or four inches of clearance between the ground and the cockpit edges, and no one could figure out how I had crawled out of there, particularly with my parachute on. Moreover, the fighter had come down on top of a stump that extended all the way up to the floor of the cockpit in an area that would have been right between my legs. I was not injured at all. The mystery lingers to this day.'

Chamberlain's crash notwithstanding, the P-47s had by now earned a reputation for toughness and reliability, but some teething problems

Cpl John Turnblom, who was a welder with the 64th FS, won the Bronze Star for devising a fix to the problem of cowling bracket breakage that afflicted the new P-47s in the MTO. His solution was later incorporated on the Republic production line (*John Turnblom*)

remained. The solution to one of these problems lay in the skilled hands of a 64th FS welder, Cpl John L Turnblom;

'They were getting persistent breakdowns in some of the aeroplanes. The lugs that held the cowling onto the airframe were moulded into the aluminium cylinder heads of the Pratt & Whitney engines. A lot of them broke, grounding the aircraft. Republic sent three engineers to Corsica to examine the problem. Capt (Frederick) Ryan, the squadron's engineering officer, said he had a man who could weld aluminium.

'I set up my ladder and welded the broken parts. They tested the aeroplane for two days and did not have any trouble with the welding. After accepting the welding, I had 79 aeroplanes to weld! They even sent some in from other outfits. If my welding had not been up to scratch the USAAF would have had to ship all these engines back to Hartford and issue replacements. I got all the aeroplanes back in service in a short time and was awarded a Bronze Star for it.'

Two weeks of intense operations from Corsica peaked on 14 April 1944 when the 57th FG flew six missions totalling 91 sorties in the Florence-Arezzo area and rolled up such a record of damage to the enemy that the group earned its third Distinguished Unit Citation. Not only did the day's toll include destruction of two tunnels, one rail bridge, six locomotives, a large oil dump, 108 rail cars and at least five motor vehicles, but also one mission by the 64th FS P-47s engaged enemy fighters and destroyed three for no losses.

By this time it had become obvious to the men of the 57th FG that the people of Corsica – a French possession – were not all that happy to be hosting them on their island. Thievery and vandalism were commonplace, even after the P-47-equipped Free French unit GC 2/5

Capt Paul Carll, C Flight commander in the 64th FS, was flying P-47D 'No 22' on a dive-bombing mission near Arezzo, Italy, on 14 April 1944 when his flight engaged 32 enemy fighters over Lake Bolsena. In the fight that followed, Carll was credited with two Bf 109s destroyed. Later that summer, after Carll had rotated home, another pilot was shot up in 'No 22' on a bridge-busting mission and crash-landed the fighter at Alto, on Corsica (*Lyle Custer*)

joined the 57th at Alto to learn fighter-bomber tactics. Nevertheless, the men enjoyed living at a pleasant camp site in the mountains several miles from the air strip, safe from the occasional night raids by Luftwaffe bombers. Most slept in pyramidal tents, but the more ingenious men built fairly comfortable lodgings out of discarded drop tank and ammunition boxes. After Rome fell to the Allies in early June, personnel occasionally could get rest passes to visit the great city or the picturesque Isle of Capri near Naples.

Although the flying was dangerous and at times frightening, most pilots found fighter-bomber work satisfying. Capt Lyle H Duba of the 65th FS, in a letter to the author, recalled a mission during June 1944 when his squadron was supporting the invasion of the island of Elba (located just off the Italian coast) by French colonial forces;

'During the invasion of Elba we received a report that our troops were being heavily shelled by artillery positions on the Italian coast. We went out there and spotted the guns, dive-bombed them and stopped the shelling. We got a "thank you" from the ground commander. It made us feel like we were doing some good. Another time off Corsica, we took off before dawn and flew up the Italian coast looking for shipping. I spotted five vessels – a cruiser and four destroyers. We dive-bombed but the results were poor. Had one hit and a small fire, but no serious damage to the ships. I had never seen such flak though. Those five ships really threw up the stuff, including cables on parachutes that we had to dodge. Maybe that was why our bombing was not too great on this occasion.'

Duba completed 129 missions before being posted back to the US in August 1944.

Allied anti-aircraft guns put on an impressive show of firepower over Corsica in response to a night raid by Axis bombers during the summer of 1944. Personnel of the 57th FG lived in tents several miles from Alto Landing Ground in an attempt to stay out of harm's way (*Gerald Schwartz*)

The group headquarters personnel of the 57th FG gathered for a photographer at Alto, Corsica, in May 1944. P-47D 'No 60' 42-75640 in the background was the regular mount of Capt Francis 'Spanky' Manda of the 65th FS. Manda, squadron operations officer, was shot down in the aeroplane in January 1945 and spent the rest of the war as a PoW (*Herbert Arnold*)

Another veteran pilot in the 65th FS at that time was 1Lt Jim 'Wabbit' Hare. He recounted to the author further development of fighter-bomber tactics during the summer of 1944;

'At Alto we began to receive eight- to eleven-second delay fuses for our high-explosive 500- and 1000-lb bombs. The powers that be decided we could be more accurate in cutting the rail lines from low altitude – that is, from below 500 ft. Yep, we could and did, and after a few missions we started dropping the bombs singly in order to get more cuts. That meant putting your pipper a tad left of the tracks if you were dropping the bomb on the right wing, and vice versa.

'After we proved the effectiveness of this system, our operations officer (Maj Dick Hunziker) decided that maybe we could skip-bomb

Maj Richard O Hunziker points to the 'Thunderbomber' design he painted on the tail of his P-47D 'No 61' 42-75724. Hunziker fought a long war in the 57th FG, scoring a victory during the Palm Sunday 1943 mission shortly after joining the 65th FS, and continuing to fly until VE Day. He was promoted to group operations officer in the summer of 1944 (*John Hunziker*)

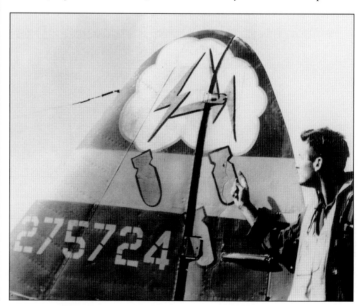

railway tunnels. I was a flight commander, and my flight was selected to be the "Tunnel Busters". The other three members of the team were Stephen B Secord, element leader, and wingmen (Burton) "Andy" Andrus and (Herbert) "Tommy" Thomas. We flew at least 20 of these hair-raising missions on the deck, strafing the target, dropping a single bomb and then immediately going into a high-G pullout to avoid the ridge the tunnel went through. On several occasions the bomb exited the other end of the tunnel before exploding, but most of the time it detonated inside. I feel certain that we caught several locomotives hiding inside, thinking they were safer than safe. Before we finished that project, the Armed Forces newspaper *Stars & Stripes* published an article and photo of my tunnel-busting flight.'

A big party was planned on 1 July to mark the beginning of the 57th FG's third year overseas. Flight operations were cancelled for the afternoon and Maj Gen John K Cannon, now Twelfth Air Force commander, arrived to lead the festivities. But the fireworks actually started in the morning when a 66th FS formation returning from a dive-bombing mission encountered an estimated 15 Bf 109s south of Reggio Landing Ground and downed six of them with no losses. It is likely the enemy aircraft belonged to the *Aeronautica Nazionale Republicana* – the reformed fascist Italian air force. Top scorer on the day was Lt Howard W Cleveland with two victories, while single kills were credited to Lts Stephen L Bettinger, Thomas D Davis Jr, Richard L Johnson and Claude G Rahn. Bettinger would become an ace while flying F-86s in Korea during 1953.

Deliveries to the 57th FG of new P-47Ds with bubble canopies began during the summer of 1944 while the group was still on Corsica. Here, P-47D-28 'No 81' 42-29307 of the 66th FS jettisons its two 500-lb bombs into the Tyrrhenian Sea just off Alto. The men of the 57th FG figured that the Allies must be winning the war when they saw new aircraft being delivered to them uncamouflaged! (*Gerald E Smith*)

Groundcrews of the 66th FS pose with P-47D 'No 87' 42-26421 *Thunderbomber*. Barely visible below the cockpit is a victory flag marking the aerial success of regular pilot Lt Thomas D Davis Jr over a Bf 109 on 1 July 1944. The aeroplane was also marked with an oval badge between the squadron number and the fuselage vent denoting it as Republic Aviation Corporation Employees War Bond Plane 45 (*New England Air Museum via Mark O'Boyle*)

One of the more colourful P-47s in the 57th FG was Lt Jim Hare's 'No 44' 42-75719 *WICKED WABBIT*. Hare's younger sister designed the bunny cartoons that graced both sides of the fuselage. He had the distinction of scoring the 65th FS's last aerial victory of the war when he shot down a Caproni Ca.133 on 7 July 1944 (*Dwight Orman*)

Lt Jim Hare was leading 12 P-47s of the 65th FS assigned to attack fuel dumps and rail tracks in the Po Valley on 7 July. He recalled it as one of his most memorable missions;

'We got some good hits on suspected fuel dumps but no outstanding fires. We made a few cuts in the rails, strafed a few vehicles and were searching for more when someone called on the radio, "Bogey at 'one o'clock low!'" I saw a black dot moving northwest at about 200 ft above the ground, seemingly unaware of our presence. The dot soon became an aircraft about ten miles ahead of my formation.

'I transmitted on my radio, "I have him". Every pilot in the formation had him by then and poured on the coals, and it became a race to see who would get there first. I think I had the advantage of making the decision to go after the bogey and got to full throttle first. None of the fellows could catch me, and as I got closer I recognised the bogey as an Italian transport aeroplane. My fighter was going so fast that when I got in range the Ca.133 was almost like a stationary target. I realised I would have time for just a one-second burst at most before overshooting him.

'I put my gunsight pipper barely in front of the nose of the target and squeezed off my one-second burst of eight 0.50-cal machine gunfire. The poor guy probably never knew what happened. His aeroplane exploded into a ball of flame and plunged 150 ft into the Po River. All the pilots on the flight slowed down to cruising speed and we flew back to our field on Corsica.

'I really looked forward to showing off my spectacular kill with my gun camera film but was sorely disappointed when our gun camera technician, Sgt Francis E Hudlow, informed me that all the film in my "No 44" *WICKED WABBIT* had been used up by the previous pilot flying the aeroplane. Well, no film but 11 good witnesses.'

Jim Hare had no way of knowing it at the time, but he had scored the last confirmed aerial victory for the 65th FS in World War 2, bringing the squadron's grand total to 49 German and Italian aircraft shot down. His long service in the 57th FG began in August 1943 on Sicily, and he flew 169 missions before returning to the US on leave

Identical twins Elbert and Richard Adams, both armourers, served together in the 65th FS. Here, they service the guns on Lt Jim Long's 'No 59' 42-25725, which previous pilot Ken Gustavson had named *Yin Fiss*. Note the bazooka tubes for 5-in aerial rockets, which were introduced to the 57th FG in late July 1944. 'No 59' was shot down on 27 February 1945, killing pilot Lt William H Anderson (*Jim Long*)

Particularly effective against
so-called 'soft' targets such as
aircraft and troops on the ground
were these fragmentation bomb
clusters (*Jim Long*)

in October 1944. Hare returned to the group and flew an additional
24 sorties before war's end, including another memorable one in which
he was forced to ditch his P-47 in the Adriatic Sea and was picked up
by a Walrus ASR crew. His last job in the 57th FG was assistant group
operations officer.

Life began to drag for the men of the 57th FG as midsummer 1944
arrived, but the arrival of a film crew headed by noted Hollywood
director William Wyler gave them a new distraction. The USAAF had
sent Wyler to make a movie about the 57th FG's role in Operation
Strangle, which the brass in Washington was touting as a major success.
Further studies of Operational *Strangle* after the war produced less

Maj Gil Wymond and his P-47D
'No 40' 42-27910 *Hun Hunter XIV*
became movie stars when
Hollywood director William Wyler
brought a crew to Alto in July 1944
to shoot the movie *Thunderbolt*.
Note the P-47 features yellow wing
and tail bands (a 57th FG standard
marking), but the black borders on
the bands have yet to be added.
Wymond was on his 16th *Hun
Hunter* (44-21035) by war's end
(*New England Air Museum via
Mark O'Boyle*)

glowing reports of its effectiveness, but Wyler's crew nevertheless shot thousands of feet of glorious colour film at Alto during a visit that lasted several weeks. Ultimately, Wyler produced a film titled *Thunderbolt*. The group commander, Col Archie Knight, was credited as technical advisor, and the stars of the film were Maj Gil Wymond and his pilots of the 65th FS.

The film told the story of a day in the life of a fighter-bomber squadron on Corsica, and included stunning footage of the 'Fighting Cocks" P-47s in the air and on the ground. To this day, historians and scale modellers study it frame by frame to discover subtle details of the Thunderbolts' distinctive markings.

SOUTHERN FRANCE

About the time Wyler's film crew was wrapping up its work, rumours began to circulate that the Allies were soon to invade southern France. The 57th FG and other Twelfth Air Force units flew several missions into the area during early August, harassing lines of communication and assessing the enemy fighter strength, which turned out to be minimal.

The invasion took place on 15 August 1944, with pilots and groundcrews of the 57th rising early to send off their first missions before dawn. By 0730 hrs, five flights from each of the squadrons were in the air, dive-bombing gun positions and patrolling over the beachhead. The group kept up operations at this pace for several days, and on 18 August the 66th FS suffered the tragic loss of veteran pilot

A Cleveland Tractor Company Medium M2 High-Speed Tractor, popularly known as a 'Cletrac', tows 65th FS P-47D 'No 49' 42-76022 at Alto during the summer of 1944. This Cletrac is fitted with a crane attachment and winch on the front that were likely to have been used for changing engines in P-47s (*Jim Long*)

Howard Cleveland. Squadronmate Joe Angelone recalled Cleveland's death, and his own close call, in a letter written for the squadron newsletter in 2005;

'It was my sixth mission, an armed reconnaissance into southern France, and my radio was dead for the entire flight. I recall strafing a long supply line of horse-drawn wagons. It was sort of sickening to hit the horses head-on with eight 0.50-cal machine guns and observe them rearing up in their tracks. Thank God I never had to do it again.

'When we returned to Alto there was a complete coverage of thunderstorms. We left the area and headed for Italy, and I was very concerned as I was low on fuel. By the time we arrived at our destination, which was a long dirt strip for B-24s, I was really hurting for fuel and my radio was still dead. (Lt James) Fleming somehow got out of his flight position in the landing sequence and landed immediately in front of me. Cleveland was in front of him and had stopped on the runway. I later learned he did this because he was awaiting taxi instructions. Fleming landed a little long and hot, and he ran into Cleveland's aeroplane, scattering debris everywhere.

'My landing gear and flaps were down, and I felt I could easily land and stop before getting to the wreckage, but the tower gave me the red light so I poured on full power and aborted the landing. The low-fuel-level light came on, but I kept the power up until I could get the landing gear and flaps up and reach a safe bailout altitude. I sucked the power back and finally got a green light, landed and stopped well short of the wreckage. My ship took a full tank of fuel upon refuelling, I had been on fumes!

'I was "tail-end Charlie" on the flight and was Cleveland's wingman, thus I was the last man scheduled to land and was probably the lowest on fuel. How Fleming ended up between Cleveland and me instead of in an earlier landing position is beyond me. I took a strong lesson from this experience – always clear the runway as quickly as possible and don't trust anyone behind you. I observe that to this day.'

The only 57th FG pilot to down an enemy aeroplane over France was Lt Bobby J Pridgeon of the 66th FS, who was one of five pilots on an armed reconnaissance along the Rhone River on the afternoon of 19 August. The P-47s strafed a convoy of 35+ vehicles, about half of which were tanks and half-tracks, destroying three and damaging eight more in two passes. As the Thunderbolts came off the second strafing pass, three Bf 109s dove on them from 6000 ft out of the sun. Lt Pridgeon pulled up into the enemy aircraft and shot down one of them.

With southern France quickly secured and the US Seventh Army moving steadily forward, the assumption around Alto was that the 57th FG would soon be moving from Corsica to France. That turned out not to be the case. On 3 September the 57th FG was ordered to turn its attention back to the Italian front, flying missions in support of Allied troops facing the Gothic Line.

Then on 9 September 'A' Party departed for Grosseto, in Italy, to prepare the recently captured Ambrone Landing Ground for the arrival of the full group. The party boarded a vessel in the nearby harbour in Calvi and was surprised to see that for the first time since departing the

Groundcrews prepare P-47s of the 65th FS for their next mission at Alto during the summer of 1944. Nearest to the camera is Lt Homer Wilson's 'No 58' 42-75767 *Shirley*, while third in line is the camouflaged P-47D-25 'No 64' 42-26754 assigned to Lt O J 'Ty' Cowart, named *Hi Mr Jackson* on the port side and *Adele K* (for crew chief Frank Roewer's wife) to starboard (*Dwight Orman*)

Ranger more than two years prior, the 57th FG would be making the trip on a ship manned by the US Navy. 'B' Party arrived on 21 September, but by that time heavy rain had turned Ambrone into a sea of mud, rendering it unsuitable for P-47 operations. The Thunderbolts were flown to the nearby main airfield at Grosseto, which had a concrete runway, on 25 September. The 57th FG would operate from Grosseto, which is located on the west coast of Italy about 100 miles north of Rome, until the closing days of the war.

Although bad weather greatly restricted flying during the 57th's first weeks back in Italy, the 65th FS nevertheless suffered a severe blow during this period. On 29 September, the squadron's rooster mascot 'Uncle Bud' was crossing a road on the airfield when he was run over by a Jeep and killed. His loss was mourned by the men of the squadron, who gave him a proper burial. It soon became obvious that the bird's absence was hurting squadron morale, so CO Gil Wymond wrote a letter to cartoonist Milton Caniff asking him to assist the 65th FS in getting a replacement.

Caniff, who had drawn the squadron badge before the 65th FS departed overseas, put a mention of 'Uncle Bud's' demise in his nationally syndicated cartoon strip, *Terry and the Pirates*. Hal P Monahan of Lake Placid, New York, whose son Hal Jr had been killed while flying with the 65th FS in December 1943, saw the comic strip and decided to sponsor the new 'Uncle Bud'. Republic Aircraft purchased the rooster and handed it over to two 65th FS pilots (Capts Ray Donahue and James Eubanks) returning from leave in the US, and they smuggled the bird to Grosseto. 'Bud II' survived the war and

101

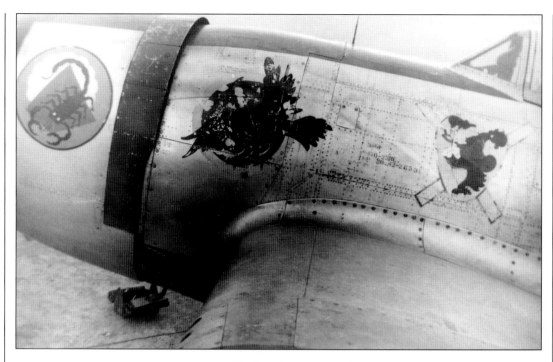

Col Archie Knight, 57th FG commander in 1944-45, carried on in the Salisbury tradition by displaying the three squadron badges on his well-worn P-47D-25 'No 01' 42-26531 (*Al Welbes*)

eventually found his way to the South Dakota farm owned by the parents of Capt E H 'Duke' Ellington. Finally, an 'Uncle Bud III' rooster would serve in the 65th FS in Alaska during the early 1950s.

Despite the bad weather limiting operations, the 57th FG lost three P-47s during October 1944. But the weather took a different swipe at the group on 2 November when a rain-weakened dam broke in the hills north of Grosseto. The resulting flood inundated the airfield and cut off the group living area. SSgt George Coyle of the 66th FS procured a fishing boat, which was rigged to a cable-crossing powered by a truck winch and used to ferry men out of the flooded camp area. The enlisted men moved into villas near the beach where the officers had been living, and the officers moved to a large farmhouse.

When flying resumed a few days later, operations picked up a faster pace that would intensify in the coming months. Now the mission shifted back to interdiction of enemy supply routes behind the Gothic Line. New weapons arrived at Grosseto for the Thunderbolts, including fragmentation clusters and fire bombs.

Operation *Bingo* kicked off on 6 November with the objective of knocking out the electrified rail line transformers in the Brenner Pass through the Alps at the border between Italy and Austria. Soon the 'Thunderbombers' were attacking locomotives and rolling stock up and down the line. Pilots of the 66th FS reported the most intense flak they had ever seen during a strike by 16 P-47s against Trento that week.

The 64th FS flew its 900th mission of the war on 10 November, sending seven P-47s to attack a railway bridge with 500-lb bombs. The attack cut the tracks north and south of the bridge, and then the P-47s strafed three track vehicles and a staff car, noting one 'flamer'. A formation of friendly twin-engined bombers was nearby, and the 64th

FS pilots spotted a single Bf 109 at 14,000 ft stalking the bombers. The operations report described what happened next;

'Our formation was at 7000 ft. The enemy aircraft turned off from a dive at the bombers into our formation, who boxed him in. Five of our pilots procured strikes on it, and he dove smoking onto a hedge, where he blew up and disintegrated afire.'

This was to be the squadron's last confirmed aerial victory of the war, and credit was divided between Capts Frank Boyd and Paul Hall and Lts Lawrence Grace, John Anderson and George Anderson.

The pilots were not the only personnel exposed to excitement and danger at Grosseto. Consider this day – 30 November 1944 – in the life of Lt David S Ketchum, armament officer of the 66th FS;

'I was working "on the line" as usual, supervising my armament and ordnance crews in arming the next flight. Several of us noticed that instead of landing, a flight of P-47s returning from a mission kept

Capt Paul M Hall had a share of the 64th FS's last aerial victory of the war. Shown here with his P-47D 'No 32' *Dixie Gal*, Hall was leading a flight of seven Thunderbolts on 10 November 1944 when they encountered a lone Bf 109 and boxed it in, five pilots sharing credit for shooting down the fighter. Hall completed 133 missions and was serving as squadron operations officer when the war ended (*Carl Lovick*)

circling the field. Suddenly Maj Leaf (squadron commander) appeared, stated that he had been in the control tower supervising the landings, and that one of the 64th FS's P-47s had a "hung" 500-lb bomb that could not be dropped from the air. Finally, as the aeroplane – and the entire flight of 12 P-47s – began to run out of fuel, its pilot was ordered to land.

'As feared, the moment that aeroplane hit the ground the bomb was released, and it tumbled nose over tail down the runway at an initial speed of about 100 mph. It finally stopped in the centre of the only runway at Grosseto, and the group commander was unwilling to order the rest of the flight to land, although fuel supplies were low. The 64th FS was unable to produce a man of experience in bomb disposal,

Lt William Harse of the 64th FS showed a sense of humour when he named his P-47D 'No 18' 42-29021 *Harse's Arse*. Harse, D Flight commander, completed 91 missions during the war and went on to serve 14 years on active duty. After a tour as a USAF test pilot, he left the military to join Convair (later General Dynamics) as an engineering test pilot on the F-102, F-106 and F-111 (*William Harse*)

and Maj Leaf asked me if I would take over. I drove by Jeep to the centre of the runway. The area was cleared of all personnel and vehicles, and the incoming aeroplanes kept circling overhead. Meanwhile, another flight had arrived over the field. There was commotion in all directions, but I had no crowd problems on the runway beside the bomb.

'A quick glance showed that both nose and tail fuses were so badly mangled that the normal procedure for returning them to the 'safe' position was out of the question. The only thing that could be done – unsophisticated as it sounds – was to unscrew the twisted metal from each end of the bomb and hope that this could be accomplished without disturbing the firing mechanism, which now had to be considered as "armed". After some awkward moments the task was completed and flares rose from the tower announcing that the runway was clear and could now accept landings. The rest of the P-47s landed safely.'

The squadrons averaged about 90 missions and 600+ sorties during the month of December. On the 13th of that month the 64th FS flew its 1000th mission of the war – a dive-bombing attack on an enemy barracks compound led by Capt Mike McCarthy. The 66th FS took the brunt of the combat losses, including four in one day, and Lt Ken Lewis counted himself lucky not to have been amongst them. He penned this account of his sortie on 14 December in his diary;

'Flew my 12th mission today and thought for a while that it was going to be my last one. Target was a bridge in eastern Italy, above the Adriatic Sea. Went up over the overcast, pulled out over the water, let down and went on to the target area under the overcast. Flak over the target was moderate, and we bombed with good results.

SSgt Gerald Schwartz, a crew chief in the 66th FS, poses in the cockpit of his P-47D 'No 73' 44-20116 *Queen Anne/"AY CHIUHUAHUA"* – its regular pilot was Lt Ken Lewis. Schwartz was one of the long-service personnel offered a transfer after VE Day so that they would not have to go with the 57th FG to the Pacific. Ironically, the group arrived back in the US before Schwartz did (*Gerald Schwartz*)

'I was flying No 2 position on (Lt Charles) McCreary's wing in our eight-ship show. After our dive-bombing run we pulled up, looking for strafing targets and observed several trains running along the track some distance away. "Mac" and I got two engines on the first two trains, the rest of the flight hitting the train itself. Then we went down and strafed some tank cars on a siding, and left a number of them burning. We pulled up again and saw a large marshalling yard in the middle of a fair-sized town. I can't recall the name of the town just now. Anyway, in these yards were "beaucoup" trains and engines, so down we went.

'All this time we had been drawing intense ground fire – machine gun and 20 mm. On this pass "Mac" got another engine and I got another one too, which made four for us. Just as I pulled off my strafing pass, I really got hit by some 20 mm stuff – one burst just behind my cockpit, one in the belly of the aeroplane and one in the ammo boxes in my right wing. I knew I'd been hit and looked at my wing to check the damage. My heart came right up in my throat at what I saw. I'd been hit by incendiaries, and a fire was raging like a blast furnace inside my ammunition boxes in the wing.

'I pushed the throttle wide open to get some precious altitude and called "Mac" to tell him I was in trouble. Together, we headed for the coastline so I could bail out in relative safety. By this time the ammunition was beginning to explode in the wing and in my guns, blowing chunks out of the top of my wing. The fire has become a raging hell, melting away the guns and the uppersurface of the wing. The ship was becoming more difficult to handle all the time. I was getting pretty damned scared and was praying as hard as I knew how.

Lt Charles McCreary, a flight leader in the 66th FS, flew P-47D 'No 96' 42-29060, which he nicknamed *Mummy II* for his wife. McCreary, who led wingman Ken Lewis home from a rough mission on 14 December 1944, wrecked this aeroplane while landing at Grosseto on 7 February 1945 (*El Geva McCreary*)

'We were over the coastline now, and I was convinced I would have to bail out soon. So I opened the canopy and unbuckled my seatbelts, ready for a quick trip over the side. I wasn't too much in favour of opening that canopy with all that ammunition exploding not six feet away, but it had to be done. The fire had spread nearly to the wingtip, and I was just waiting for it to burn off completely before I bailed out. I didn't want to leave as long as the aeroplane was still flying, so, scared as I was, I rode it out. "Mac" contacted ASR and told them I planned to bail out, and gave them our position. They made arrangements to get an aeroplane out quick to pick me up, while the rest of the flight would circle around to keep the Jerries from coming out after me.

'Most of the ammo had exploded by now, and the wing still stayed on. I began to have faint hopes of the fire burning itself out. I slipped and skidded the aeroplane to bring more wind to bear on the fire, and after a few more agonising minutes the fire flickered and died! So there I was, 200 miles from home but with just a burned-out shell of a right wing. She didn't fly so well, but she was still up there with the engine turning over okay, so the rest of the flight formed up around "Mac" and me, and we headed home.

'I carefully tested the aeroplane on the way home and found that although I had no right aileron, I could still control her pretty well. The wheels and flaps still worked, and my spirits started picking up considerably. Finally we reached the home field, and I made an emergency straight-in landing. Brought her in for a wheel landing, and that nerve-wracking flight was over!'

In mid-December the entire group moved into downtown Grosseto to be closer to the airfield, as enemy air attacks were no longer a threat.

A mixed formation of 57th FG Thunderbolts circle over an island off Grosseto, Italy, in late 1944. The fighters are, from left to right, 'No 25' 44-33106 of the 64th FS, 'No 3' 44-33052, which was a group headquarters aeroplane maintained by the 64th FS, 'No 80' 42-28046, flown by Lt Bud Kranzush of the 66th FS, and 'No 59' 42-25725, which was Lt Jim Long's *Yin Fiss* of the 65th FS. 'No 3' and 'No 59' both went down on operations in 1945 (*John Hunziker*)

The squadrons of the 57th FG celebrated their third Christmas overseas in parties at Grosseto on 25 December 1944. Here, seven pilots of the 64th FS line up for a portrait. They are, from left to right, George or John Anderson, operations officer Mike McCarthy, squadron commander Bob Barnum, Bruce Hale, Paul Hall, J M McLaughlin and Gerald Brandon (*Carlton Chamberlain*)

The officers took over a hotel and the enlisted men were housed in a separate building. A convoy of trucks carried interested personnel to Rome on Christmas Eve to take in midnight mass at the Vatican, and they returned the next morning in time for turkey dinners in the officers' and enlisted messes, followed by open houses in the respective clubs.

A little weary after celebrating the 57th FG's third Christmas overseas, the men returned to a full schedule of operations on 26 December. A USO show that evening, featuring baseball stars of the 1944 World Series, brought the Christmas season to an exuberant close. On the last day of the year, Maj Charlie Leaf had the honour of leading the 66th FS on the group's 3000th combat mission – an uneventful dive-bombing show in the Massa area. Several weeks later, Leaf would become the first 57th FG pilot to reach the milestone of completing 200 combat missions.

January 1945 was notable for its on-again-off-again weather. Missions were now focused on the Brenner Pass, and it seemed that if the weather was suitable for operations in the target area, it would be bad at Grosseto, and vice versa. Nevertheless, the 57th FG continued to pound enemy targets, completing 229 missions that month. As veteran pilots reached 100 missions and were sent home tour-expired, a steady stream of replacements arrived at Grosseto. Lt David P Black joined the 65th FS at this time and was fortunate that there were still veteran pilots

around to show him the ropes. He recounted his steep learning curve in a 2002 letter to the author;

'Fighter-bomber tactics were always get in and out as fast as you could. When attacking trains, shoot the engine first to stop it, then come across at 90 degrees, shooting at each car. Pull up early in case the train explodes. Road traffic was much the same. For troop concentrations, use fire bombs and spread them around, coming across the area in four-ship formations to maximise the coverage.

'My most memorable missions were the first three that I flew. On the first, I was "tail-end Charlie" in an attack on a sugar factory in the Parma area. I dropped bombs, shot rockets and fired my guns at the building and close-in ack-ack. Why they put guns next to the building I'll never understand. A milk run. Next morning to the Po River and a pontoon bridge. Pulled up from my bomb run and watched my flight leader, (Capt Frank) "Spanky" Manda, catch fire and bail out. Watched him to the ground, not knowing what to do. Very unnerving (Manda was captured).

'The next afternoon I was "tail-end Charlie" on an eight-ship mission to the Brenner Pass. We were escorting B-25s and dive-bombing rails. But the weather was bad, and we returned to our secondary target, the Bologna rail yards. We could see through holes in the clouds, and all followed down in trail. As I broke under the clouds at 1500 ft I got hit by an 88 mm round and turned upside down (bombs still on). I got turned

Lt David Black of the 65th FS paints the name *Smitty III* on his new P-47D 'No 50'. He named the aeroplane in honour of his wife, who incidentally flew in the WASP (Women Airforce Service Pilots) – the first women in history to fly American military aircraft. He recalled painting the name in red to match the colour of his wife's hair. Black completed 89 missions from November 1944 through to VE Day, and came home a captain (*Jim Long*)

upright but could find no one. I jettisoned my bombs and started climbing south into the mountains. I knew the tops there were only 5000 ft or lower. In clouds I prayed, climbed to 8000 ft and headed home. I made it with some radar and radio help.

'That night I was completely "undone". I was ready to tell my CO, Gil Wymond, I was through – court martial or worse, co-pilot C-47s. Duke Ellington saw my problem and got me drunk, soooo drunk. The next morning I awoke with the chaplain leaning over me. I'll never forget his words, "Try to lie your way out of this one". And then, "You ought to try God once". I did and flew 86 more missions, and got 58 more years of life to date.'

Another 65th FS pilot, Lt Fergus Mayer, was flying his 68th mission on 27 January when he was shot down. In a 2003 letter to the author he recounted the experience;

'I was leading an eight-aeroplane flight on a mission to bomb a bridge beside Lake Como up near the Brenner Pass. On our way back to base

I spotted some trucks and, as was our practice, I took the flight down to strafe them. Apparently small-arms fire got one of my cylinders and I started losing oil. My wingman told me I was trailing black smoke, so I started to climb. I got to about 5000 ft when my engine started to freeze up and smoke began filling the cockpit. At that point I trimmed it up and bailed out without any difficulty.

'As I was coming down I saw some German soldiers in a nearby field and heard some rifle shots. I landed on a barn roof at a small farm and was helped down by the farmer and his wife. They took me in their house and offered me some soup. Shortly thereafter the soldiers came and took me under their control.

'I was taken to many places and kept in solitary confinement for the most part until I got to Germany. My main residences while in prison camp was Nuremburg and Moosburg. There were other smaller camps but I can't remember their names. I contracted lobar pneumonia while in camp and came close to dying, but I was saved by a new antibiotic called penicillin, which a British doctor somehow got a hold of. I was liberated from Moosburg on 5 May 1945. I spend some time in a hospital in Lyon, France, and was then sent home.'

Like many servicemen returning to civilian life, Mayer took advantage of the GI Bill to complete his education. He graduated from medical school in 1951 and practised medicine in Des Moines, Iowa, for 31 years before retiring.

Operations continued to intensify in February, which also brought a rare encounter with enemy fighters that actually saw the P-47s come out on the short end of the score.

The eighth of 15 missions flown on 4 February was an eight-aeroplane flak diversion by the 66th FS in support of B-25s attacking a bridge at Piacenza. The mission report tells what happened;

'Our formation split to cover the two largest groups of bombers. En route to the target 15+ Me 109s and Fw 190s attacked one section of four aircraft from out of the sun at 23,000 ft, diving northwest toward our formation, which was at 13,000 ft. Nine attacked the leader and his wingman. The leader followed two down and came into range at 5000 ft. He saw strikes, and pieces flew off both aircraft. One went into the overcast at 1500 ft at a 45-degree angle. Lt Carl Weisenberg claims one Me 109 damaged. His wingman, Lt Guilford D Groendycke in aircraft "No 78" (42-29344) did a split-S and was seen to hit the deck. His aircraft exploded and burned.

'Six enemy aircraft attacked the second element leader. The wingman turned into them and called the element leader, telling him to do likewise. The element leader pulled straight up. The wingman turned left, causing the enemy aircraft to split up. He then joined the other section. The element leader, Lt Edward J Palovich in aircraft "No 79" (42-29034), was not seen again.'

The US Fifth Army began a new offensive in early March and broke the stalemate in Italy. Now, the fighter-bombers would mix close-air-support missions with interdiction in the Brenner Pass, and again the pace of operations picked up. One technique used during this period was the use of 'Rover Joe' ground controllers to help pinpoint the fighter-bomber strikes ahead of the advancing troops.

Capt Wayne Dodds of the 66th FS was the regular pilot of 'No 94' 44-21023, named *'C'est La Guerre'* on the port side and *"QUE PASA"* on the starboard (in black with a yellow outline) in the spring of 1945. He was shot down in P-47D 42-29041 on 9 December 1944 but was able to avoid capture and return to combat flying. In 1985, Dodds published a history of the 57th FG titled *The Fabulous 57th Fighter Group of World War II* (*New England Air Museum via Mark O'Boyle*)

The controller, usually a veteran fighter-bomber pilot on detached duty, would set up shop in an armoured car at a spot overlooking the frontlines and radio target assignments to the P-47s overhead. These missions proved extremely effective. Also coming into use at about this time was 'Auntie' radar-controlled bombing, which was used with questionable success to allow the P-47s to drop their bombs through the clouds when overcast obscured their targets. Bill Berry, a veteran flight leader with the 64th FS, describes how 'Auntie' missions worked;

'A radio call to "Auntie" would initiate the first step, and we would make a couple of turns so "Auntie" could make a positive ID on our flight. "Auntie" would then specify an exact course, exact air speed and exact altitude for our flight. Minor one- to two-degree course corrections would be made, followed by, "Prepare to drop; one, two, three, DROP". Flying a tight formation, every pilot released his bombs. I just happened to be the first flight leader to need "Auntie's" expertise with radar, but unfortunately I had not briefed my wingman, flying his first mission. Everything worked perfectly until the word "DROP". The new guy did an immediate split-S and dived down through the overcast. A half-hour after we landed he made it back and wanted to know what the hell was going on. We were told we had a good pattern on target.'

Losses continued to mount despite the employment of these new technologies. Dave Hutton, a veteran flight leader in the 66th FS, recalled a remarkable squadronmate who went down during this period in correspondence with the author in 2003;

'I first became friends with Miller Anderson while in advanced pilot training at Eagle Pass, Texas. Prior to the war, he was in his sophomore year at Ohio State, where he had received a scholarship for his prowess as a diver on the swimming team. He had been recognised as the top diver in the US, and was fully expected to be the number one diver on the Olympic team, but Pearl Harbor put an end to his career and

he was called to service. We went from Eagle Pass to Florida State University (FSU), then to Waycross, Georgia, for overseas training in P-40s. While in ground school at FSU, whenever we had a break we went to Wakula Springs and the Crystal Clear Lake, which had diving boards and platforms. Andy (as he was called) put on diving exhibitions, and people would watch spellbound as he did his flips, twists and rolls from the high platforms.

'We went to Italy and were both assigned to the 66th FS on Corsica. From there we went to Grosseto. On 21 March 1945 Andy was on his 65th or so mission when he was shot down by ground fire after making his bomb run. The P-47 was hit deep over enemy territory and he was seen to parachute down. We thought Andy had probably been captured by the Germans. Later, we got a report that he had been found in a hospital in Bologna and was sent back home for his recovery.

'We heard no more about him until the end of the war. I returned to my college, Miami University in Oxford, Ohio, in October 1945. Sometime in 1953 I was on a business trip to Columbus, Ohio, and looked up Andy. I met him for dinner and caught up his activities since we had our last contact the day he was shot down in 1945. He told me that after being hit by ack-ack he bailed out and his left leg was fractured when it was struck by the horizontal tail section. He was picked up by the Germans and taken to a field hospital, where they put a cast on his leg. He was then moved to a hospital in Bologna, where he stayed until the area was taken over by Allied forces. He was sent back

Lt Dave Hutton of the 66th FS poses with his trusty P-47D 'No 74' *War Weary*, while armourers Titgemeyer and Pinkham work on the guns. Hutton recalled that 'No 74' was the last razorback P-47 in the squadron, and probably flew 200 or more missions before it was retired in the spring of 1945. At this writing, Hutton keeps the 'Exterminators' in touch as the editor of the 66th FS newsletter, *Calling Jackpot* (*Dave Hutton*)

113

Lt George Blackburn poses with the second P-47D he flew in the 66th FS, *"Sweetheart"* (44-20873). Lt Miller Anderson was flying this aeroplane on 21 March 1945 when he was shot down and taken prisoner. Blackburn took over Anderson's 'No 77' *Lena Mae* shortly thereafter and nearly went down himself when he was hit in the wing and engine on a mission (*George Blackburn*)

to the US, where doctors told him his leg had not been properly set. They had to re-break and reset it.

'After a period of rehabilitation he was released from service, went back to Ohio State and rejoined the diving team. Andy had to learn to "take off" from his right leg because his normal take-off leg never regained full strength. He made the 1948 and 1952 Olympic teams and won silver medals in springboard diving both years. He said *Look* magazine ran an article on him. I think it was published in 1947 or 1948. He started building home swimming pools after graduation and would put on diving exhibitions for his customers to celebrate their pool openings. He remained in the business until his early death in the late 1960s or early 1970s. He was good man and friend, and I enjoyed regular visits with him over the years.'

The 57th FG made its last claims for air-to-air combat on 26 April 1945, and again it was the 66th FS 'Exterminators' that found themselves in the middle of it. The group flew no fewer than 33 missions that day, and on the 20th one, two P-47s of the 66th FS were assigned to operate under the control of 'Rover Joe' near the frontlines. The P-47 pilots, Capt Richard L Johnson and Lt Roland E Lee, were strafing a vehicle when a lone Bf 109 attacked them. The operations report follows;

'The Me 109 came from the northeast and made a pass at Lt Lee, but was out of range. The Me 109 then made a second pass and Lt Lee made an evasive turn. The enemy aircraft then started a third pass, but Capt Johnson cut him off. Capt Johnson's guns failed, but he kept the enemy aircraft in his sights for about one minute. At about 3000 ft,

the enemy aircraft pulled up and was nearly in a stall, then made a split-S to the right. Lt Lee first fired from about 1500 ft, and was about 500 ft away when the Me 109 was hit between the cockpit and the tail. The pilot jettisoned his canopy and bailed out (dark green 'chute). The enemy aircraft then did three rolls up, tumbled and spun in. Lt Lee followed it down and fired two bursts as it hit the ground. The

Lt Dwight Orman's 65th FS P-47D 'No 65' 44-21014 *Duration Dotty* is hung with 500-lb bombs and rocket tubes in preparation for a mission during the closing days of the war. Next in line is Lt Jim Long's 'No 59' 44-33093 *Blitzy*. Orman and Long were avid photographers and created a marvellous visual record of the pilots and aeroplanes of their 'Fighting Cocks' squadron (*Dwight Orman*)

Capt Dick Johnson, operations officer of the 66th FS, would almost certainly have scored the 57th FG's last aerial victory of the war on 26 April 1945 had his guns not failed during a dogfight with a Bf 109. After riding the enemy fighter's tail for about a minute, Johnson moved aside so his wingman, Lt Roland Lee, could make the kill (*New England Air Museum via Mark O'Boyle*)

Here are two photographs taken the same day of 65th FS P-47D 'No 53' (44-20866) bombed up for a mission to northern Italy, showing the name *Schmaltzie* on the port side and *Mercedes* to starboard. Lt Francis Middleton was the regular pilot of this aeroplane, but Lt Leonard R Hadley was shot down in it on 25 April 1945 and listed as killed in action (*Dwight Orman*)

aeroplane broke into pieces but did not explode. The Me 109 had yellow bands around the nose, its fuselage was dark and camouflaged, the wings had rounded tips and were adorned with German crosses.'

With this final kill, the 57th capped its air-to-air score for the war at 184 enemy aircraft confirmed destroyed, 20 probables and 79 damaged.

The 57th FG suffered its last combat casualty on 29 April 1945. Lt Aikens V Smith, a flight leader in the 65th FS, turned away from his formation near Florence for no apparent reason and did not

respond to radio calls. He was found sometime later, having bailed out but apparently been killed when he struck the tail of his P-47D 42-19586.

As April (the busiest month in the long history of the group) came to a close, the 57th FG moved north out of Grosseto and took up residence at the recently captured Villafranca airfield near Verona. By the time the group set up shop and was ready to resume operations, however, all missions were called off because no valid targets remained in Italy. The 57th FG moved back to Grosseto but flew no further missions before 8 May – the date when the Allies formally accepted the unconditional surrender of the armed forces of Nazi Germany. The long war of the 'First in the Blue' 57th FG was over.

The exploits of the pilots who flew in the 57th FG earned them a prominent place in the history of World War 2, and rightfully so. They faced the ultimate risk and deserved all of the accolades they received. But it is important to remember that no fighter aeroplane could leave the ground without the efforts of a whole cast of people who made that possible.

The following is excerpted from the Orders of the Day issued on 1 July 1944 by group commander Lt Col Archie J Knight on the second anniversary of the 57th FG's departure from the US. Although written

Lt Col Charlie Leaf leads the 66th FS in his olive drab P-47D 'No 70' 43-26752 in a flight over Grosseto in April 1945. Squadron commander Leaf, who had served in the RAF prior to joining the 57th FG in early 1943, became the first pilot in the group to complete 200 combat missions in early 1945 (*John Hunziker*)

Crew chief Eugene Schnabel takes a break on the wing root of P-47D 'No 02' 44-20342 *Jeeter*, which he maintained for Lt Col W J 'Jeeter' Yates, deputy group commander. The aeroplane displays a list of the campaigns in which Yates, one of the original *Ranger* pilots, participated in during his two combat tours in the 57th FG. Yates was elevated to group commander after VE Day, and brought the group home from Italy aboard the *Sea Owl* (*New England Air Museum via Mark O'Boyle*)

A happy Lt Jim Long of the 65th FS waves goodbye to Grosseto on 1 July 1945 as he prepares to board the group's B-25 hack for the first leg of his trip back to the US. Long completed 78 combat missions, joining the squadron in July 1944 and staying on operations through to the end of the war (*Jim Long*)

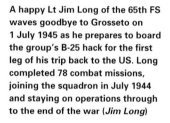

some ten months before the end of the war, it sums up the contributions of the 'First in the Blue' ground personnel through to VE Day very well;

'It was ours to pave the way for units to follow, ours to be the first "Yanks in the Blue". To follow a trail that back then appeared to have no end. The true story can be recorded by the sweat, guts and determination of that little-known band of men who made the group the world-famous organisation it is today. The story of the crew chiefs, armourers and radio men whose day began before first light and often extended into the night with the aid of a flashlight. The story of the cooks who made bully and M&V into a variety of more edible forms. The story of the pencil

pushers and red tape. The story of the truck drivers whose long hauls brought bombs, ammo, petrol, water, rations and "Vs" to the group. The story of a task well done.'

POSTWAR

The men of the 57th FG did little celebrating at Grosseto on VE Day. They were happy the war in Italy was over, but they were still a long way from home. On 6 June 1945 came news that caused morale to drop like a bomb – the 57th FG had been chosen to deploy as a unit directly to the Pacific, presumably to take part in the upcoming invasion of Japan. The spirits of some rose considerably two weeks later when it was announced that the longtime veterans, many of whom had served in the 57th since its arrival in North Africa, would be reassigned to units returning to the US.

On 6 August 1945, the transport ship *Sea Owl* departed from Naples with the 57th FG on board, destination somewhere in the Pacific. Then on 14 August, as the ship was nearing South America, word came that Japan had surrendered. The *Sea Owl* turned north the next day and arrived in Boston four days later. The 57th FG was inactivated on 7 November 1945.

The 57th FG was not gone for long. It was reactivated at Shemya, Alaska, on 15 August 1946, flying the P-51H Mustang before transitioning to the jet-powered F-80 Shooting Star and F-94 Starfire. It was inactivated again in 1953 but came back a third time in 1969 as the 57th Fighter Weapons Wing. At this writing, the 57th Wing provides fighter training at Nellis AFB, Nevada.

When the 57th FG was reactivated in Alaska during 1946, it inherited P-38s and P-51Hs from the deactivating 343rd FG. *Mickey Finn 3rd* (44-64424) was a P-51H-5 assigned to the 65th FS, as designated by the AB squadron code. The colour of the wing and tail bands is not known (*George Poole*)

APPENDICES

APPENDIX 1

UNIT COMMANDERS OF THE 57th FIGHTER GROUP

Group Commanding Officer

Capt John E Barr	15 January 1941
Maj Reuben Moffat	Spring 1941
Maj Clayton Hughes	19 August 1941
Maj Minthorne Reed	12 December 1941
Lt Col Frank H Mears	28 June 1942
Lt Col Arthur G Salisbury	23 December 1942
Lt Col Archie J Knight	23 April 1944
Lt Col William J Yates	25 May 1945

64th Fighter Squadron

Capt Romulus Puryear	15 January 1941
Capt Frank H Mears	19 August 1941
Capt Clermont E Wheeler	28 June 1942
Capt Glade S Bilby	20 August 1942
1Lt Arthur E Exon	17 August 1943
Capt Louis Frank III	20 April 1944
Maj Robert A Barnum	24 October 1944

65th Fighter Squadron

Capt Philip G Cochran	15 January 1941
Capt Arthur G Salisbury	28 June 1942
Maj Gordon F Thomas	23 December 1942
Capt Gilbert O Wymond	12 May 1943
Capt Edward H Ellington	29 May 1945

66th Fighter Squadron

Capt G C Russell	15 January 1941
Capt Peter G McGoldrick	19 August 1941
Capt Lyndon King	20 November 1941
Maj Charles R Fairlamb	28 June 1942
Capt William J Yates	21 February 1943
Maj James G Curl	15 May 1943
Maj Glenn A Reich	18 August 1943
1Lt William P Benedict	13 December 1943
1Lt Cortland McCoy Jr	5 June 1944
Maj Charles G Leaf	9 July 1944

APPENDIX 2

DISTINGUISHED UNIT CITATIONS OF THE 57th FIGHTER GROUP

I.

'Cited for outstanding performance of duty against the enemy on 18 April 1943. On this date, at a time when operations in northern Tunisia were reaching their culminating intensity, 47 Warhawks of the 64th, 65th and 66th FSs of the 57th FG and the 314th FS of the 324th FG, escorted by a top cover of Spitfires of the Royal Air Force, were despatched on a fighter sweep over the Gulf of Tunis for the purpose of attacking enemy aircraft in the Cape Bon area. In the course of the patrol, a large force of approximately 100 three-engined enemy transports of the Ju 52 type, escorted by 50 Me 110s, was sighted six miles off the coast flying in close formation low over the water. The Warhawk pilots immediately engaged the enemy formation, swooping down from 8000 ft into the midst of the troop-laden transports and wreaking a devastating toll on their numbers.'

II.

'Cited for outstanding performance of duty in action against the enemy in direct support of the British 8th Army in the long-running Middle East campaign, from the battle of El Alamein to the final capitulation of the enemy forces in Tunisia and Sicily. The group, operating from a series of advanced airfields directly behind the frontlines under the most difficult of desert weather and terrain conditions, carried out continuous and devastating dive-bombing and strafing raids against enemy aerodromes, ground installations, troops and supply lines (both on land and at sea), as well as many fighter patrols and fighter escorts for their own and Allied bombardment aircraft. The group also engaged in repeated aerial engagements with large formations of enemy aircraft, in which vast numbers of enemy aircraft were destroyed.'

III.

'Cited for outstanding performance of duty in armed conflict with the enemy. Pioneering in the adaptation of the high-altitude P-47 as a low-level strafing and dive-bombing aircraft, the 57th FG perfected these techniques to such a high degree of effectiveness that on 30 March 1944 the group was moved from the Italian mainland to Corsica to operate as a separate task force. Selected to accomplish the interdiction of rail and road routes and the destruction of locomotives, rolling stock and motor vehicles behind enemy lines, the group was directed to provide a minimum of 48 fighter-bomber sorties per day and customarily to furnish its own top cover. Displaying outstanding efficiency and zeal in surpassing these requirements, the unit, during its nine days of combat operations from 1 to 14 April 1944, exceeded an average of 80 sorties per day. On 14 April 1944, the 57th FG distinguished itself through extraordinary heroism, determination and *esprit de corps* in a flawlessly coordinated group effort which struck a series of devastating blows to the enemy in the Florence-Arezzo area. Flying 91 sorties between 0810 hrs and 1610 hrs, the pilots of this group, in six consecutive missions, destroyed two tunnels, one railway bridge, six locomotives and a large oil dump. More than 13 trains were attacked, 108 rail cars destroyed, damaged or set on fire and tracks were cut at nine different points. Five motor vehicles were strafed and left burning and ten others were destroyed or damaged. With all missions briefed to engage any hostile aircraft sighted, one formation of 16 P-47s attacked more than 32 Me 109s and Fw 190s, destroyed three, probably destroyed a fourth and dispersed the remainder. Near Ponarance, 16 other Thunderbolts strafed 40 barracks-like buildings, and through flames and explosions which hurled debris to a height of 4000 ft, repeatedly attacked these installations until 25 buildings had been hit and 19 fires started, which threw flames 500 ft into the air. From the day's operations, one aircraft is missing and three returned to base with battle damage.'

APPENDIX 3

BASES OF THE 57th FIGHTER GROUP, 1941-46

1941

15 January	Activated at Mitchell Field, New York, USA
19 August	Day Field (renamed Bradley Field), Windsor Locks, Connecticut, USA
8 December	Group HQ and 64th FS, East Boston, Massachusetts, USA
13 December	65th FS, Trumbull Airport, Groton, Connecticut, USA
14 December	66th FS: Republic Field, East Farmington, New York, USA

1942

24 January	65th FS, Rentschler Field, East Hartford, Connecticut, USA
1 June	66th FS, Hillsgrove, Rhode Island, USA
1 July	Quonset Point, Rhode Island, USA
30 July	Muqueibila, Palestine
27 August	66th FS, Maryut, Egypt
2 September	66th FS, LG 97, Egypt
7 September	66th FS, Maryut, Egypt
16 September	LG 174, Egypt
6 October	66th FS, LG 91, Egypt
5 November	Group HQ, 64th and 65th FSs, LG 172, Egypt
	66th FS, LG 106, Fuka, Egypt
7 November	66th FS, LG 101, Egypt
7-9 November	Group HQ, 64th and 65th FSs, LG 75, Egypt
11 November	66th FS, LG 76, Egypt
11-13 November	Group HQ, 64th and 65th FSs, Sedi S'Azeiz and Gambut, Libya
12 November	66th FS, Gambut, Libya
15 November	Group HQ, 64th and 65th FSs, Air el Gazela, Libya
	66th FS, LG 150, Libya
19 November	LG 3, Gambut, Libya
2 December	Belandah No 1, Libya
4 December	Belandah No 2, Libya
31 December	Hamreit, Libya

1943

19 January	Bir Dufani, Libya
22 January	Darragh West, Libya
23 February	Zuara, Tripolitania, Libya
2-5 March	Mefatia South LG, Tunisia
6 March	Mefatia Main, Tunisia
9-11 March	Ben Gardane, Tunisia
20-21 March	Soltane, Tunisia
1 April	Hasbub, Tunisia
4 April	Hasbub North, Tunisia
5-11 April	Cekhira, Tunisia
14 April	El Djem, Tunisia
15 April	El Hani, Tunisia
20 April	Kairouan, Tunisia

APPENDICES

21 April	El Djem, Hani Main and El Aowanta, Tunisia
1 May	Hani Main, Tunisia
20 May	A Party, Bou Grara, Tunisia
6 June	El Haoaria, Cape Bon, Tunisia
19 June	Causeway, Tunisia
7 July	Tripoli Staging Area, Libya
13 July	Luqa and Gozo, Malta
20 July	Panchino, Sicily
31 July	Scordia, Sicily
18 September	Rocco Bernardo, Italy
25 September	Gioia del Colle, Italy
2 October	Foggia No 8, Italy
6-8 October	Foggia No 1, Italy
25 October	Amendola, Italy

1944
| 16 January | Arcola, Italy |

1 March	Cercola (Naples), Italy
24 March-2 April	Alto, Corsica
9 September	Ombroni (Grosseto), Italy
11 September	Grosseto Main, Italy

1945
29 April	Villafranca di Verona, Italy
7 May	Grosseto Main, Italy
15 July	Staging Area No 3, Bagnoli, Italy
18 August	Camp Miles Standish, Boston, Massachusetts, USA
20 August	Drew AAB, Tampa, Florida
7 November	Inactivated

1946
| 15 August | Reactivated, Shemya, Alaska |

APPENDIX 4

57th FIGHTER GROUP PILOTS EMBARKED IN USS *RANGER* (CV 4), JULY 1942

(Total of 72 pilots and P-40Fs)

Headquarters
Maj Frank Mears, CO
Capt Harry French
Capt Archie J Knight

64th FS
Capt Clermont Wheeler, CO
1Lt Robert A Barnum
1Lt Glade B 'Buck' Bilby
1Lt Tracy W Smith
2Lt William S Barnes
2Lt Robert W Beals
2Lt William S Beck
2Lt Gerald A Brandon
2Lt Ernest D Hartman
2Lt Nicholas P Harvey
2Lt Frank E Hertzberg
2Lt 'Mac' McMarrell
2Lt Lyman S Middleditch
2Lt George D Mobbs
2Lt William J Mount
2Lt William M Ottoway
2Lt R J 'Jay' Overcash
2Lt Gordon L Ryerson
2Lt Jack S Wilson

65th FS
Capt Arthur Salisbury, CO
1Lt Thomas W Clark
1Lt Horace W Lancaster
1Lt Delvert V Mitchell
1Lt William W O'Neil
1Lt Marshall Sneed
1Lt Gordon F Thomas
1Lt Roy E Whittaker
1Lt Gilbert O Wymond
2Lt Edward H Ellington
2Lt Arnold D Jaqua
2Lt Richard B Kimball
2Lt Leo B Margolian
2Lt Robert L Metcalf
2Lt James L Morris
2Lt Robert N Nichols
2Lt Walter H Reed
2Lt Harold C Rideout
2Lt Harry H Stanford Jr
2Lt Edwin R Weaver

66th FS
Capt. Charles R Fairlamb, CO
1Lt James G Curl
1Lt Raymond A Llewellyn

1Lt George W Long
1Lt Richard E Ryan
1Lt William J Yates
2Lt Robert M Adams
2Lt Ralph M Baker
2Lt Joe D Bell
2Lt Thomas M Boulware
2Lt Lewis L Bowen
2Lt William R Campbell
2Lt Arlie W Claxton
2Lt Dale R Deniston
2Lt James T Gardner Jr
2Lt Robert E Gibson
2Lt John T Gilbertson
2Lt Harry J Hayden
2Lt Robert A Hoke
2Lt Richard B Paulsen
2Lt Alan H Smith
2Lt John J Stefanik
2Lt William E Taylor
2Lt John E Teichrow
2Lt Thomas M Tilley
2Lt Thomas T Williams
2Lt William B Williams
2Lt Albert Zipser
2Lt Charles S Zucker

COLOUR PLATES

1

P-40B (serial unknown) of the 64th PS, Day Field, Windsor Locks, Connecticut, USA, August 1941

Although the 57th PG was activated in January 1941, it did not get aircraft or pilots until the spring of that year. In the meantime, 57th PG mechanics gained experience by working with 8th PG groundcrews on their machines. This P-40B was one of the first assigned to the 64th PS/57th PG. Devoid of personal markings, it carries only the standard national insignia of the period, plus the unit designators on the fin. It is likely that the aeroplane participated in the 57th's ill-fated deployment from New England to the West Coast in October 1941.

2

P-40E 41-5726 of Capt Philip G Cochran, 65th FS CO, East Hartford, Connecticut, USA, April 1942

This colourful P-40E displays the first known application of a squadron badge on a 57th FG aircraft. It was assigned to the 65th FS commander, Capt Phil Cochran, as denoted by the twin command stripes around the fuselage. Cochran arranged for noted cartoonist Milton Caniff, a friend from college days, to design the 65th FS 'Fighting Cocks' badge, which shows an aggressive red rooster with a chip on his shoulder and a shamrock hanging around his neck. Cochran did not deploy to North Africa with the 57th FG, but he gained fame later as a squadron commander in Tunisia with the 33rd FG and then as co-commanding officer of the 1st Air Commando Group in Burma. Caniff portrayed him as character 'Flip Corkin' in his popular *Terry and the Pirates* comic strip.

3

P-40F-1 41-13911 of the 64th FS/57th FG, USS *Ranger* (CV 4), July 1942

This is believed to be the first Warhawk lost by the 57th FG in Africa. Flown by 1Lt Tracy W Smith, it was one of 72 aircraft that launched successfully from the *Ranger* on 19 July 1942 on the first leg of the long trip across the continent to Egypt. The next day, 1Lt Glade B Bilby wrecked 41-13911 at Accra, in British West Africa, when he caught a wingtip in a crosswind landing. As crew chief Herb Gluckman observed of Lt Bilby in his diary entry that day, 'Is he pissed off!!' Aircraft 'No 12' fails to show up in 64th FS mission reports throughout the next few months of combat, leading to the assumption that *JO* was indeed the aeroplane wrecked at Accra. 'Buck' Bilby went on to post an outstanding combat record, however, scoring 3.5 aerial victories and serving as 64th FS commander for nearly a year.

4

P-40F-1 41-13878 of 2Lt Thomas T Williams, 66th FS, LG 97, Egypt, 4 September 1942

Red propeller spinners and white fuselage numbers were added to the 57th's P-40Fs during the last week of August 1942 to aid in aircraft recognition. This Warhawk had a noteworthy, if short-lived, operational history with the 66th FS. One of the original complement of *Ranger* aircraft, 'No 77' was flown off the carrier by 2Lt John E Teichrow, carrying the name *Lucy* on the starboard side of the nose at that time. It was the mount of 2Lt Thomas T

Williams on 4 September 1942 – the day he scored the first allowed claim by a USAAF pilot in the Middle East (a Bf 109 probably destroyed while escorting bombers over western Egypt). On 28 October 1942, future ace 2Lt R J 'Jay' Overcash was flying this P-40 when he downed a Bf-109F to score the first of his five victories. 'No 77' flew its 35th, and last, combat mission on 11 November 1942, and it was condemned on 8 December.

5

P-40F-1 (serial unknown) of Maj Charles R Fairlamb, 66th FS CO, Maryut, Egypt, September 1942

Maj 'Fuzzy' Fairlamb commanded the 66th FS during its first six months of combat operations. His P-40F-1, 'No 70', is shown here as the fighter appeared in late September 1942 after its propeller spinner was painted red – a standard DAF marking. The red flash and diamond behind the spinner was a carry over pre-war 57th FG marking, and Fairlamb's name was the only personal adornment applied to the aircraft. 'No 70' was heavily damaged in a forced landing on 22 October 1942 after it sprung a glycol leak and the engine overheated. A popular leader, Fairlamb completed at least 48 combat missions before being badly burned in February 1943 when the stove caught fire in the officers' mess tent at Darragh West, in Libya. Upon recovering from his injuries, Fairlamb became an instructor at the replacement training unit at El Kabrit, in Egypt.

6

P-40F-1 (serial unknown) *Miss Fury!* of 1Lt Roy E Whittaker, 65th FS, LG 174, Egypt, October 1942

1Lt Whittaker named his P-40F-1 after a popular female comic strip superhero of the period, '*Miss Fury*', who was notable for her skin-tight panther costume and her fighting skills. Whittaker scored his first confirmed victory in this aircraft when he shot down a C.202 south of El Dabr on 28 October 1942. He went onto record seven confirmed victories, making him the top-scoring ace of the 57th FG. In mid-November 1942 this aircraft was reassigned to the 66th FS at Martuba as 'No 96'. 1Lt John T Gilbertson was flying it on 13 December 1942 when he downed a Bf 109F near Agheila.

7

P-40F-1 (serial unknown) *The Shadow* of 2Lt A Wade Claxton, 66th FS, Martuba, Libya, November 1942

Named for the mysterious title character in a popular radio serial, *The Shadow* was one tough Warhawk. 2Lt Wade Claxton, its first assigned pilot, flew the aeroplane on 20 missions between 2 September and 17 November 1942 before being wounded. Claxton required a three-month convalescence, so 'No 72' passed to Lt Adrian Stahl. The aeroplane stayed in action throughout the North Africa campaign, completing 115 missions with 25 different pilots and accounting for four confirmed victories before the Axis surrender in May 1943.

8

P-40F-1 (serial unknown) *???/Heil Heel* of the 66th FS, Belandah No 2, Libya, December 1942

One of the first replacement aircraft received by the 66th FS, the devilish 'No 74' was flown most often by Lt Tom Tilley before he transferred to the 64th FS in mid-November 1942. The aeroplane completed 51 sorties but went down on 23 January 1943, having fallen victim to ground fire during a dive-bombing mission. Pilot Lt Bob Minett of the recently arrived 79th FG, flying with the 66th to gain experience, belly-landed the aeroplane behind enemy lines and returned to base unhurt with the help of friendly Arabs.

9

P-40F-1 *UNC A BUD* of Capt Marshall Sneed, 65th FS, Bir Dufani, Libya, 20 January 1943

Sneed, a flight commander in the 65th FS and one of the original *Ranger* pilots, named his Warhawk for the squadron's mascot, a feisty rooster brought to North Africa from the US named 'Uncle Bud'. The subject of the rudder art is unconfirmed. A minor league baseball player before the war, Sneed was credited with a confirmed victory on 20 January 1943 in *UNC A BUD*, but neither he nor the rooster survived the war. Sneed was shot down over the Bay of Gabes on 22 February 1943 and 'Uncle Bud' was run over by a Jeep in 1944.

10

SM.79 (serial unknown) of 2Lt William P Benedict, 66th FS/ 57th FG, Darragh West, Libya, February 1942

Benedict, who joined the 66th FS in January 1943 after flying Spitfires with the RAF, was a legendary scrounger. With the help of Lt Charlie Leaf, he located this nearly intact SM.79 at Castel Benito and decided it would make a good addition to the squadron. With the help of several mechanics, Benedict and Leaf returned the aeroplane to airworthiness and flew it back to Darragh West, where it acquired USAAF markings. 'The Green Goose', as the plane was called, made supply runs and ferried personnel for several weeks until the lack of spare parts grounded it. Benedict and Leaf would both command the 66th FS later in the war.

11

P-40K-1 42-46040 of Capt R J 'Jay' Overcash, 64th FS, Tunisia, May 1943

The circulation in 2008 of a colour photograph taken by *Life* magazine photographer Hart Preston near the end of the North African campaign revealed previously unknown details about the markings on this ace's aircraft. Of particular interest is the rudder art, showing a fez from the famous Savoy Hotel in Cairo, and the Morse Code inscription dot-dot-dot-dash ('V for victory') below the exhausts. The P-40K's tan top colour is well worn, revealing the Olive Drab factory paint in various places, particularly around the wing roots. Jay Overcash scored his fourth and fifth victories, both Bf 109s, in this aeroplane on 26 April 1943.

12

P-40F-20 41-20019 of Capt Dale R Deniston, 66th FS, Gozo, Malta, July 1943

By mid-1943, late model P-40Fs and P-40Ls such as this one began replacing the 57th FG's ageing short-fuselage P-40Fs and P-40Ks. Capt Dale Deniston of the 66th FS flew 'No 80' during the aerial campaigns over Pantelleria and Sicily during the summer of 1943. One of the original pilots who flew off the *Ranger*, Denison completed 100 sorties from 19 July 1942 through to 14 August 1943,

when he was rotated home. He went on to make a career of the USAF and retired with the rank of colonel.

13

P-40F-10 41-14597 *'NOBBY'* of 1Lt Louis Mastriani, 64th FS, Scordia, Sicily, August 1943

Lou Mastriani arrived in Africa with the 324th FG in early 1943 and ferried a P-40 from Accra, Gold Coast, across the continent to Cairo before being transferred to the 57th FG in March. In the following year he flew 92 combat missions, winning a DFC plus an Air Medal with 6 oak leaf clusters. Mastriani's 'No 18' P-40F only carried the name *'NOBBY'* (his brother's nickname) for its first few missions. 'I was hit by flak on two consecutive missions', he recalled. 'After that, I decided to remove the name'.

14

P-40L-1 42-10453 of 1Lt Paul L Carll, 64th FS, Scordia, Sicily, September 1943

Paul Carll was a replacement pilot who joined the 64th FS in Tunisia shortly after the end of the fighting in North Africa and went on to become a flight commander in the squadron. In addition to RAF-specification dark earth/middlestone camouflage, the aeroplane has yellow-bordered national insignias on its fuselage sides. This was Carll's second P-40, and the first of three personal aircraft (the other two were P-47s) to carry the squadron number '32'. Carll scored three confirmed victories, including a pair of Bf 109s shot down over Italy on 14 April 1944.

15

P-40F-15 41-19851 of 1Lt William F Livesey, 66th FS, Rocco Bernardo, Italy, September 1943

Bill Livesey was a former RCAF pilot who transferred to the USAAF in December 1942. He took part in the famed Palm Sunday 1943 mission and came back with credit for 3.5 Ju 52/3ms destroyed and one damaged. Livesey went on to complete 134 combat missions and returned home to New Jersey in time for Christmas 1943, but he was killed in an aeroplane crash in 1946. Note the red border on 'No 93's' national insignia, which 57th FG aircraft carried for several months in the autumn of 1943.

16

P-47D-15 42-75648 of Capt Alfred C Froning, 65th FS, Amendola, Italy, January 1944

Capt Froning became the 57th FG's last ace when he shot down two Bf 109s over the coast of Yugoslavia on 16 December 1943 for his fourth and fifth confirmed victories. At the time of the action, the P-47 he was flying was so new that its fuselage number had not yet been applied. This design of the 65th FS badge, on a white disc with the rooster facing the rear of the plane, would change in the months ahead. When Froning finished his combat tour, Lt John Wittenberger was assigned to 'No 51' and its crew chief, SSgt Don Williams. On 5 September 1944 Wittenberger hit high-tension wires while strafing near Milan in this P-47 and crashed to his death.

17

P-47D-15 42-75724 *JOANNE* of Capt Richard O Hunziker, 65th FS, Amendola, Italy, April 1944

Dick Hunziker began his combat career with the 65th FS in April 1943, just in time to score a Bf 109 destroyed on the

Palm Sunday mission. A year later he was A Flight commander, flying this Thunderbolt, and he commanded the squadron during May-June 1944 before becoming the 57th FG operations officer. Hunziker had completed 200 combat missions by the end of the war, and he subsequently enjoyed a distinguished career in the USAF, retiring with the rank of major general in 1969.

18

P-47D-15 42-75713 *Mehitabel* of Capt Louis Frank III, 64th FS CO, Alto, Corsica, May 1944
Lou Frank assumed command of the 64th FS on 20 April 1944 when Maj Art Exon was shot down and taken prisoner. Earlier that month Frank had been credited with two Italian BR.20s shot down and one damaged while leading an armed reconnaissance south of Florence, Italy. He named his P-47 for 'Mehitabel', a scrappy female cat who served as the muse for a cockroach poet in the popular 'Archy and Mehitabel' stories by Don Marquis, a columnist for *The Evening Sun* in New York.

19

P-47D-15 42-75764 *Chi Miss* of Lt George W Wilson, 64th FS, Alto, Corsica, summer 1944
Chi Miss and its pilot, Lt Wilson, were both assigned to the 64th FS in early 1944, and they both were battle-tested veterans by the time the group moved to Corsica the following spring to participate in Operation *Strangle*. Wilson was promoted to first lieutenant in June 1944 and earned his first Air Medal two months later.

20

P-47D-27 42-27179 of 1Lt R Bruce Abercrombie, 64th FS, Alto, Corsica, summer 1944
Lt Abercrombie flew in the 64th FS from mid-1943, carrying 'No 33' on a P-40F named *Ginger* and also on this P-47. He was shot down by flak north of Rome on 30 March 1944 but was able to ditch safely off the coast and be picked up by an RAF Walrus. Abercrombie returned to operations shortly after catching up with the group on Corsica. He became a flight commander in June 1944 and completed his combat tour later that summer. 'No 33', which carried the name *Sandra* on the starboard side, eventually sustained damage in a belly landing.

21

P-47D-23 42-27910 *Hun Hunter XIV* of Maj Gilbert O Wymond, 65th FS CO, Alto, Corsica, summer 1944
Wymond, the long-serving commanding officer of the 'Fighting Cocks', was largely responsible for developing the P-47 into the awesome ground-attack weapon it became in the Twelfth Air Force. Another of the original pilots who flew off the *Ranger*, Wymond remarkably remained on operations throughout the war, save for a leave in May-June 1944. He eventually flew 16 different *Hun Hunters*, but this razorback is the best known because of its starring role in the movie *Thunderbolt*, filmed on Corsica by noted director William Wyler.

22

P-47D-15 42-75719 *WICKED WABBIT* of 1Lt James C Hare, 65th FS, Alto, Corsica, summer 1944
Jim 'Wabbit' Hare made the most of his limited chances to engage in air-to-air combat. On 7 July 1944, while on a

dive-bombing mission, he spotted a twin-engined Ca.133 in German markings over the Po River and promptly shot it down for his squadron's last confirmed aerial victory of the war. Hare's 'No 44' P-47D sported different cartoons of a warrior rabbit (based on a drawing by his younger sister) on each side of the fuselage, plus a large rendering of its name, *WICKED WABBIT*, on its starboard side. The B Flight badge was also added to the vertical tail when Hare became commander of the flight.

23

P-47D-25 42-26795 *Jackie 6* of Capt Howard Hickok, 65th FS, Alto, Corsica, summer 1944
Iowan Howard Hickok joined the 65th FS in 1943 and eventually became B Flight commander prior to taking leave in the US in April 1944. He was assigned this aircraft when he rejoined the squadron on Corsica, and received a DFC in August 1944. The significance of the kill marking below the cockpit is unclear, since Hickok's only aerial claim was for a Bf 109 damaged on 12 January 1944. *Jackie 6* crashed in bad weather north of Siena on 31 October 1944, killing pilot Lt George Lovato.

24

P-47D (serial unknown) of Lts George Berglund and H Harmon Diers, 64th FS, Grosseto Main, Italy, late 1944
When Lt Berglund completed his combat tour in November 1944, this well-travelled P-47D was assigned to Lt Diers, a recently arrived replacement pilot. Diers recalls that the aeroplane was referred to as 'Old 38' but did not have a name painted on it. The red tail suggests that the fighter may have been transferred to the 57th from the 332nd FG when the latter unit transitioned to P-51 Mustangs in mid-1944. Diers won the DFC for a mission on 12 April 1945 in which he made repeated attacks on a train near Milan, destroying eight rail cars and three vehicles.

25

P-47D-25 42-26765 *The Lady Jake* of Capt Edward F Jones, 64th FS, Grosseto Main, Italy, early 1945
Eddie Jones recalled that he had a rough introduction to combat flying when he joined the 64th FS in the late summer of 1944. On his first mission, the three leading Thunderbolts in his eight-aeroplane flight were brought down by a huge secondary explosion when their bombs detonated an ammunition dump. Camouflaged bubble-canopy P-47s were fairly common in the Twelfth Air Force, and Jones named his 'No 33' for his high school sweetheart, whose nickname was 'Jake'. He had completed 76 missions by the end of the war and went on to a civilian career in journalism and public relations.

26

P-47D-30 44-33092 *Blitzy* of 1Lt Jimmy R Long, 65th FS, Grosseto Main, Italy, spring 1945
Jim Long joined the 65th FS on Corsica and flew his first combat sortie on 2 September 1944. By war's end he had completed 78 missions. When Lt Long's old razorback 'No 59' *Yinn Fiss* was lost with Lt William Anderson on 27 February 1945, Long got this shiny new P-47D-30 as a replacement. His diary recorded an incident when a rocket attached to *Blitzy* accidentally fired while the aeroplane was sitting on the ground at Grosseto – 'Darned near

knocked us off the wing. It went out about two miles and, luckily, nothing was hit'.

27

P-47D-30 44-21014 *Duration Dotty* of 1Lt Dwight V Orman, 65th FS, Grosseto Main, Italy, spring 1945

When Dwight Orman arrived on Corsica to join the 65th FS, he flew many of his early missions in a 'beat up razorback' named *Jerry Jinx* ('No 43'). After progressing – in the terms of the day – from 'sprog' to 'sport' to 'old sport', he was sent from Grosseto Main down to Naples to pick up a new P-47D-30 that would become *Duration Dotty*, his personal aircraft. 'We drove up and down rows of aircraft and finally I said "Okay, I'll take that one". Pretty heady stuff, I can assure you'. Orman managed to complete 100 missions by the time the war ended.

28

P-47D-30 44-21043 *Miss Milovin II* of Capt Alvin M Welbes, 65th FS, Grosseto Main, Italy, spring 1945

Al Welbes had inherited the first *Miss Milovin*, a well-worn P-47D-15, from a tour-expired pilot and flew it until 7 March 1945 when it was shot down (Lt C L Hewitt PoW) and he got this shiny new replacement. After initially being assigned to C Flight, Welbes became D Flight commander and was promoted to captain in February 1945.

29

P-47D-27 42-26836 *"Jerrico"* of 1Lt Quentin J Goss, 66th FS, Grosseto Main, Italy, late 1944

Quentin Goss flew in the 66th FS from July 1944 to March 1945 and completed his tour with the rank of captain after 108 combat missions. His first sortie was memorable, for he was hit by flak during his dive-bombing run and had to return to Corsica with an armed 500-lb bomb hung up on his left wing pylon. On the advice of his mission leader, Leon Jansen, Goss landed the aeroplane safely. 'I remember it clearly as one of the smoothest landings I have ever made. As soon as the aeroplane stopped rolling, I got out and ran. Years later I learned my intrepid mission leader had gotten out of his aeroplane and was in a ditch when I landed!'

30

P-47D-23 42-28046 *"Anna May"* of 2Lt Eugene D Kranzush, 66th FS, Grosseto Main, Italy, late 1944

The first of three Thunderbolts assigned to Bud Kranzush, 'No 80' was fitted with replacement tail surfaces from a Free French P-47D while the 66th was still on Corsica. It was named for his future wife, Anna May Snyder, whom he married in May 1946. Kranzush completed 95 combat missions between 16 November 1944 and 1 May 1945. He won the DFC for leading a successful dive-bombing mission against a heavily defended alcohol refinery at Bondero, in Italy, on 3 April 1945.

31

P-47D-28 44-20107 *"TOOTS"* of Capt Joseph Angelone, 66th FS, Villafranca Di Verona, Italy, April 1945

Joe Angelone started flying combat missions in August 1944, and was assigned his own aircraft – a P-47D-25 – fairly soon thereafter. The aeroplane had less than 100 hours on it when Angelone blew a tyre on take-off and wrecked it. This profile depicts the replacement 'No 71'.

Angelone named both aircraft for his mother, whose nickname was *'Toots'*. The name *'Lil Abner'* on the starboard side referred to the aeroplane's armourer, Homer Duchon, who bore a striking resemblance to the cartoon character. Angelone completed 120 operational sorties before receiving rotation orders on 6 May 1945. He became a test pilot after the war.

32

P-47D-30 44-20342 *"Jeeter"* of Lt Col William J Yates, 57th FG deputy commander, Grosseto Main, Italy, spring 1945

'Jeeter' Yates flew throughout the North African campaign with the 66th FS, serving as squadron commander from February through to May 1943 and scoring 1.75 confirmed aerial victories. Returning to the 57th FG in the spring of 1944, he became deputy group commander and went on to complete 200 combat missions. Yates ascended to group commander after VE Day. As Joe Angelone recalled of Yates, 'He would fly with the (66th) Squadron whenever he flew a mission, and he always picked a big, rough one – no everyday runs for him'.

COLOUR SECTION

1

This P-47D of the 64th FS came to grief on landing at Alto, on Corsica, during the summer of 1944. 'No 39' was named *It's We Three Virginia* in blue on the port side, but the fighter's regular pilot is unknown (*Jim Hare via www.57thfightergroup.org*)

2

Lt Jim Eubanks of the 65th FS was a Texan, and he appropriately named his 'No 41' (42-76005) *Doggie* for the steers of his home state. Note the chipped yellow paint that apparently was applied to the canopy frames of the aircraft early in its life. The 65th had not yet switched the colour of its fuselage numbers from white to light blue when this photograph was taken (*Jim Hare via www.57thfightergroup.org*)

3

P-47D 'No 50' 42-75739 *Pudgy The Flying Hangover/EL RANCHO* was one of the most colourful razorback Thunderbolts in the 65th FS. Lt William Bateman was killed in action while flying the aeroplane on 18 August 1944 (*Jim Hare via www.57thfightergroup.org*)

4

With the snow-capped Alps in the distance, P-47D 'No 77' 42-28532 sits quietly at Villafranca during the 57th's short stay there in early May 1945. In the background are an L-5 Sentinel liaison aircraft (left) and a C-47 Skytrain transport (*Jim Hare via www.57thfightergroup.org*)

ACKNOWLEDGEMENTS

For nearly a decade I gathered material for this book from veterans of the 57th FG and their families. They sent me letters, diaries, documents, photographs and even a few personal manuscripts, published and unpublished. I deeply appreciate receiving these contributions, and the faith shown in me to create an accurate and reasonably complete account of the 57th's long war in the MTO. The bibliography below lists the many secondary sources that helped provide structure and substance to this volume, and I am indebted to the creators of those works as well. In particular, I would like to give credit to Mark O'Boyle, webmaster of www.57thfightergroup.org, for all the help he has given to me. Mark and his sister Kate created this excellent site in honour of their father, Lt Kenneth J O'Boyle, a former A-20 pilot who served as flying control officer for the 57th FG in 1945.

BIBLIOGRAPHY

ANDRADE, JOHN M, *US Military Aircraft Designations and Serials Since 1909.* Midland Counties Publications, Earl Shilton, Leicester, 1979

CHANDLER, MAJ PORTER R, *The 66th Fighter Squadron, From Alamein to Tunis.* unpublished manuscript, 1943

COMPTON, CHARLES B, *Born to Fly.* Charles B Compton, North Highlands, California, 2002

DENISTON, COL DALE R, *Memories of a Combat Fighter Pilot.* Dale R Deniston, Lake Wales, Florida, 1995

HESS, WILLIAM N AND MCDOWELL, ERNEST R, *Checkertail Clan - The 325th Fighter Group in North Africa and Italy.* Aero Publishers Inc, Fallbrook, California, 1969

LONG, JIMMIE R JR, *Tales From the Fighting Cocks' Roost.* Jimmie R Long Jr, Williamsburg, Virginia, 1997

MOLESWORTH, CARL, *Osprey Aircraft of the Aces 43 - P-40 Warhawk Aces of the MTO.* Osprey Publishing, Oxford, 2002

RING, HANS AND SHORES, CHRISTOPHER, *Fighters over the Desert.* Arco Publishing Co Inc, New York, 1969

RUST, KENN C, *Ninth Air Force Story.* Historical Aviation Album, Temple City, California, 1982

RUST, KENN C, *Twelfth Air Force Story*, Historical Aviation Album, Temple City, California, 1975

SCHOENFIELD, ALBERT, *The Saga of the Exterminators Squadron.* Direct Imaging, San Luis Obispo, California, 1994

SCUTTS, JERRY, *Osprey Aircraft of the Aces 2 - Bf 109 Aces of North Africa and the Mediterranean.* Osprey Publishing, Oxford, 1994

WAGNER, RAY, *American Combat Planes.* Doubleday & Co Inc, Garden City, New York, 1968

INDEX

References to illustrations are shown in **bold**. Colour Plates ('pl.') and Colour Section ('cs.') entries are shown with page and caption locators in brackets.